"We live in a culture that constantly demands more of women. Y[ou]
are not exempt from this pressure. In fact, this is the time—in [our]
twenties—when we're just beginning to fall prey to the increa[...]
school, social media, smartphones, relationships, work, and b[...]
barely out of childhood and already feeling overwhelmed, [...]
pressed, drowned, and burned out. That's why we need the joy[...]
of the gospel of grace. And that's exactly what Shona and [...]
deliver in *Refresh*. They write warmly, empathetically, biblic[...]
cally. I will be applying the wisdom of this book to my own m[...]
recommending it to the young women I know!"

> **Jaquelle Crowe,** lead writer and editor in chief, TheRebelution.com;
> contributor, The Gospel Coalition; author, *This Changes Everything*

"I have searched high and low for a book that helps me deal with stress-related illness in a God-honoring way. I have stacks of books that either overspiritualize depression and stress-induced illness or overmedicalize it. I struggle with balance, and I need help. To the rescue comes *Refresh*, a book that meets you where you are, preaching neither overspiritualized idealism nor worldly fatalism. Read this book and give it to friends. It will change the way you see God's providence in your emotional suffering and physical weakness, and it will encourage you on a path of self-care that honors the Lord and enables you to serve your family of God for the long haul."

> **Rosaria Butterfield,** former professor of English, Syracuse University;
> author, *The Secret Thoughts of an Unlikely Convert*

"Shona's transparency and gentle coaching throughout this book provide the perfect context for the encouragement that *Refresh* will be to many women who have experienced burnout or are on the verge of burnout. As a counselor and a woman who has experienced it, I appreciated the holistic approach to both the causes of burnout and its treatment. The Murrays fully address both body and soul in their book, which will leave you refreshed, renewed, and ready to lead others alongside streams of living water flowing from the Great Shepherd of our souls."

> **Heather Nelson,** biblical counselor; author, *Unashamed: Healing Our
> Brokenness and Finding Freedom from Shame*

"Burnout and exhaustion are not solely a female issue, but as a woman I can attest to experiencing these very things in recent years. The demands on our time are many and coming from all directions. How will we use our time? How will we find balance? How will we maintain our walk with the Lord in the midst of so much? Shona and David Murray understand these pressures and speak directly to them in this book. Drawing on her own experience of depression and burnout (and experience as a medical doctor), Shona has a winsome and practical approach to the balance and rest we all crave (yet struggle to find). If you are desperate for relief, you will find encouragement in *Refresh*."

**Courtney Reissig,** author, *The Accidental Feminist* and *Glory in the Ordinary*

"Reading *Refresh* in a bone-weary season of my life was like having a life-giving conversation with a couple of grace-filled friends who have been there themselves and were able to encourage me with practical, biblical wisdom."

**Nancy DeMoss Wolgemuth,** author; Bible teacher; host, *Revive Our Hearts*

# ReFRESH

# ReFRESH

*Embracing a Grace-Paced Life in*
*a World of Endless Demands*

Shona Murray and David Murray

WHEATON, ILLINOIS

*Refresh: Embracing a Grace-Paced Life in a World of Endless Demands*
Copyright © 2017 by Shona Murray

Published by Crossway
    1300 Crescent Street
    Wheaton, Illinois 60187

Published in association with the literary agency of Legacy, LLC, 501 N. Orlando Avenue, Suite #313-348, Winter Park, FL 32789

First printing 2017

Printed in the United States of America

Unless otherwise indicated, Scripture quotations are from *The New King James Version*. Copyright © 1982, Thomas Nelson, Inc. Used by permission.

Scripture quotations marked KJV are from the *King James Version* of the Bible.

Trade paperback ISBN: 978-1-4335-5522-0
ePub ISBN: 978-1-4335-5525-1
PDF ISBN: 978-1-4335-5523-7
Mobipocket ISBN: 978-1-4335-5524-4

---

**Library of Congress Cataloging-in-Publication Data**

Names: Murray, Shona, 1967- author.
Title: Refresh : embracing a grace-paced life in a world of endless demands /
    Shona Murray and David Murray.
    Description: Wheaton : Crossway, 2017. | Includes bibliographical references
    and index.
Identifiers: LCCN 2017007115 (print) | LCCN 2017036670 (ebook) | ISBN
    9781433555237 (pdf) | ISBN 9781433555244 (mobi) | ISBN 9781433555251
    (epub) | ISBN 9781433555220 (tp)
Subjects: LCSH: Christian women--Religious life. | Burn out
    (Psychology)--Religious aspects--Christianity.
Classification: LCC BV4527 (ebook) | LCC BV4527 .M87 2017 (print) | DDC
    248.8/43--dc23
LC record available at https://lccn.loc.gov/2017007115

---

Crossway is a publishing ministry of Good News Publishers.

| LB | | 27 | 26 | 25 | 24 | 23 | 22 | 21 | 20 | 19 | 18 | 17 |
|----|----|----|----|----|----|----|----|----|----|----|----|----|
| 15 | 14 | 13 | 12 | 11 | 10 | 9 | 8 | 7 | 6 | 5 | 4 | 3 | 2 | 1 |

To our beloved children,
Allan, Angus, Joni, Amy, and Scot

# Contents

# Introduction

*Overwhelmed. Exhausted. Depressed. Panicky. Stressed. Burned out. Broken. Paralyzed. Drowning. Empty.* Recognize yourself in any of these words? Maybe in all of them?

You're not alone. These are the most common words I've heard Christian women using to describe themselves and their lives.

Whatever happened to the words *peaceful, calm, joyful, content, quiet, rested, refreshed,* and *fulfilled*? Wouldn't you like to exchange the second set of words for the first?

It seems impossible, doesn't it? Especially as the demands upon us keep multiplying: housework demands our energy, employers demand our hours, the church demands our commitment, friends demand our presence, kids demand our taxicab, credit cards demand our dollars, school sports demand our evenings and Saturdays, the yard demands our sweat, charities demand our donations, the sick demand our visits, marriage demands our time, relations demand our phone calls, email demands our replies, Pinterest demands our perfection, and on and on it incessantly goes.

Sometimes you want to run away, don't you? Or curl up in a ball and hide under the covers. Or jam your fingers in your ears and silence the clamor. Or maybe lock the door and throw away the key, the phone, and the ever-lengthening to-do list. The demands are simply overwhelming. And there's little prospect of change, little hope of experiencing the second group of words again, until, well, maybe retirement.

I sympathize, because I've been there too. In fact, I've probably been in a deeper and darker place than many of you, a painful story that I'll be sharing with you in the coming pages. However, over many years, and through many struggles, the Lord has graciously delivered me from the first set of words and into a more regular experience of the second. In short, he has taught me, and is teaching me, how to live a grace-paced life in a world of overwhelming demands.

## A Grace-Paced Life

A grace-paced life? What's that? It's a pace of life that's constantly refreshed by five different wells of divine grace. First, there's the *motivating* well of grace. We used to be driven by money, family perfection, beauty, careers, or earning God's favor. But instead of filling and fulfilling us, these motivations drained and dried us. Now though, we daily drop our buckets into the unsearchable depths of God's saving grace in Christ to freely receive his overflowing mercy and love. Filled to overflowing with gospel grace, we are now energized and enthused to serve him at home, at work, and at church, as our heart beats, "Thank you, thank you, thank you."

Second there's the *moderating* well of grace. Grace moderates our expectations of ourselves and others. At the foot of the cross we have seen our sin and our sinfulness. We have learned that we are not perfect and never will be. Therefore, when we fall and fail, we don't torment or torture ourselves.

Instead, we calmly take our sins to Calvary knowing that God's grace forgives us all our imperfections and lovingly accepts us as perfect in Christ. We don't need to serve, sacrifice, or suffer our way to human or divine approval, because Christ has already served, sacrificed, and suffered for us. His perfection moderates our perfectionism as we remind ourselves, "Accepted, accepted, accepted."

Third, we are refreshed by the *multiplying* well of grace. We no longer believe that everything depends on us and our efforts. Rather, we trust God to multiply our few loaves and fishes. We don't sit back and do nothing, but neither do we try to do everything. We sow and water, but we realize that it's God who gives the increase. God's blessing multiplies our work in a way that no amount of extra hours or effort can. How calming and soothing is this realization and the prayer it produces: "Multiply, multiply, multiply."

Fourth, the *releasing* well of grace helps us to hand control of our lives over to God. We trust his sovereignty not just in salvation but in every area of life. Yes, we still work diligently and carefully, but releasing grace humbly submits to setbacks, problems, and disappointments, accepting them as tests of our trust in God's control. When tempted to micromanage and dictate our lives and the lives of others, we drop our bucket into this refreshing well as we whisper to ourselves, "Release, release, release."

Finally, there's the *receiving* well of grace, which closer inspection reveals to be made up of a number of smaller wells. Each of them represents one of God's gracious gifts to his needy creatures: a weekly Sabbath, sleep, physical exercise, family and friends, Christian fellowship, and so on. In our fast-paced life we used to push these gifts away, thinking that we didn't need them. But in the grace-paced life, we approach these wells saying, "Receive, receive, receive." The more and more we see that our heavenly Father designed and drilled these wells for our good, the more we receive and enjoy their renewing and refreshing waters.

In the course of this book we'll open up these wells of God's grace and learn how and when to drink from their refreshing waters.

### Women Only?

But why write for women only? Do men not run too fast, overcommit, overstretch, and burn out too? Yes, they do, and that's why my husband, David, has written a book for men called *Reset: Living a Grace-Paced Life in a Burnout Culture*. But through personal experience and years of counseling we discovered that although there's much overlap between men's and women's experience of the stressed-to-depressed spectrum, there are also important gender-specific aspects in both causes and cures to warrant separate books. But I'd like men to read this book too, because an increased understanding of women's unique struggles will help them to serve and minister to their sisters in Christ and, together, run countercultural grace-paced lives.

I'd also encourage you to share the book with your daughters and your younger female friends, because it's not just middle-aged and older women who are feeling overwhelmed. The millennial generation (aged eighteen to thirty-three) have higher stress levels than the national average, with 39 percent saying that their stress levels have increased over the past year, 52 percent losing sleep each month due to various stresses, and 20 percent so depressed or stressed that they need medication.[1] If that's you, I have good news for you. This book will show you biblical principles, practices, and patterns that will refresh your body and your soul so that you can start living a grace-filled and grace-paced life instead of joining the statistics.

## Joint Authorship

Finally, some of you might be wondering how joint authorship works and how the content of *Reset* for men relates to *Refresh* for women. What bits did David write, what bits did I write, what bits did we write together, and how can you tell the difference? Having looked at various jointly authored books, we decided against writing *Refresh* as "we," because it's for women and, well, David is not a woman! We also didn't like the idea of switching from "I (Shona)" to "I (David)" whenever we used material from *Reset*. That just seemed awkward. Therefore, although we wrote it together, "I" (Shona) is used throughout. So what are the differences and overlaps between the two books?

First, the overall structure of the two books, the chapter headings and most of the subjects covered, are the same in both books. As David explained in his book, so much of the wisdom we have gained has come through many years of us living this together, suffering together, studying together, and counseling people together, so that our thoughts are almost identical. This similarity in structure and subjects should help husbands and wives who want to work through the books together to be on the same page, as it were, and yet also be

---

1. Sharon Jayson, "The State of Stress in America," *USA Today*, February 7, 2013, http://www.usatoday.com/story/news/nation/2013/02/06/stress-psychology-millennials -depression/1878295/.

able to identify important differences in the male and female experiences of stress, burnout, anxiety, and depression.

Second, in *Refresh* my story is substituted for David's story. In *Reset* David told of how burnout just about killed him—twice. Throughout *Refresh* I replace that with my own painful story of how I slipped into a deep hole of depression and anxiety and how God is graciously delivering me.

Third, I feminized the manly parts. Although we initially thought that we could write a book for women with just a few tweaks of the man's book, we soon realized that for all the significant similarities, there are multiple important differences in the female experience of burnout. That resulted in much more work than either of us expected, but we both agreed that it was important to make it as feminine as possible for maximum usefulness. The feminization also involved the addition of some sections that have no counterpart in *Reset*.

Although we were both a bit nervous about how to navigate a joint project such as this, as usual God surprised us and used the experience to draw us closer together and give us an ever-deeper appreciation for the beautiful complementarity of husband and wife in God's plan for marriage. Near the end of writing it, we celebrated twenty-five years of marriage and found that writing *Refresh* had been a wonderful reminder of God's goodness and mercy following us all the days of our lives. We hope and pray that you will benefit from the wisdom God has been pleased to teach us through the years and that what we have learned will refresh you, lead you into a grace-paced life in a world of overwhelming demands, and help you experience the healthy balance of grace motivation and grace moderation as exemplified by the apostle:

Therefore we also, since we are surrounded by so great a cloud of witnesses, let us lay aside every weight, and the sin which so easily ensnares us, and let us run with endurance the race that is set before us, looking unto Jesus, the author and finisher of our faith, who for the joy that was set before Him endured the cross, despising the shame, and has sat down at the right hand of the throne of God. (Heb. 12:1–2)

# Reality Check

C

I was a crumpled heap. The billows of mental pain buffeted me, leaving me barely able to breathe. I agonized over how a life that had been so full of happiness, so full of God's blessing, could become so helpless and hopeless. For five months I had fought hard against the possibility of depression. After all, part of my job as a family doctor was to help patients recover from depression. Why was I now hearing my story in their stories? Why was I so afraid to see myself in their stories?

"Only the weak get overwhelmed and burn out. Only Christians who have bad genes or have experienced a real tragedy get depression. Ordinary Christians like me don't. I must be an apostate who is depressed because God has left me. There's no hope for me. No one and nothing can fix me. Even if they could, I don't want to live without God. Yet I don't know who he is anymore. I don't know where he is. I don't see him anywhere. Why did he leave me? Will he ever rescue me? Or will I die in despair?"

My mind spun like this, minute after minute, day after day,

tortured by terrifying thoughts of God and my own tragic destiny. Until one day in March 2003 I spoke these words to my husband David through waves of tears: "I am a ship smashed against the rocks. My life is over!" Something gripped him at that moment that set us both on a course that would change our lives, a course that would eventually refresh my life and teach me how to embrace a grace-paced life in a world of overwhelming demands.

## Panic Attacks

In the months leading up to my shipwreck, I had become utterly exhausted and had completely lost my appetite. I simply had no desire to eat. One evening I tried to rest and read a book when suddenly, from nowhere, I felt a terror within, as if something awful was about to happen. My heart was pounding for no apparent reason, and I couldn't make it calm down. Over subsequent weeks I had several of these fearful episodes.

I was very sad and would cry for no obvious reason. Loneliness enveloped me even when I was surrounded by those who loved me. I became obsessional in my thoughts, sometimes inexplicably mulling over sad events for hours. The terror episodes came closer together so that I was constantly terrified. My heart would pound away, sometimes for hours. Distraction seemed the best policy, so I just kept myself busy in an attempt to run away from these strange and terrible sensations, but also because there was so much to be done.

By now my enthusiasm had gone. Diaper changes, meals, groceries, mothering two lively little boys, caring for a busy toddler, and another baby on the way became scary prospects. I dreaded the mornings, and I wanted to hide under the covers; but a strong sense of the needs of others kept me going and going and going. Weeks went by when I could hardly sleep, and I cried a lot more. Nothing interested me. I felt I was a bad mother, a bad wife, a bad daughter, and a bad Christian. Guilt over a myriad of tasks not done—or poorly done by my standards—suffocated me. And despite running at top speed, the finish line was never in sight.

## Despair Envelops

Concentrating on my devotions became increasingly difficult, and I felt that the Lord was far away. Mental exhaustion had me in its grip. One particular night as I tried to pray and kept losing track of what I was thinking or saying, I began to feel that I was falling off a cliff; I fell deeper and deeper, and there was no bottom. My whole emotional world fell apart. Through the night, I struggled between sleep and wakefulness. The most terrifying images and thoughts of God poured into my mind like an unstoppable fountain. I would respond with verses of well-known psalms, which I repeated over and over in a desperate attempt to hang on to God and his promises. I cried and cried to the Lord, but the darkness of despair descended. Like a tiny boat lost in a convulsing storm, having lost its rudder, my mind was broken, my emotions crippled, and the waves of despair plunged me down without mercy.

## No Rest

During this dark season I would sleep with exhaustion, but then awaken in an instant several minutes later, unable to stop the rage of mental torment. I concluded that the Lord had given me over to the Devil, that I could not be a Christian, and all that remained was for me to fall into hell. Long before my alarm clock went off each morning, I awoke suddenly like a startled bird. While the rest of the house slept, I had to get up, to get away from this pain. Waves of tormenting thoughts crashed on the shores of my heart: "What's going to happen to my children on the way to eternity? Who will bring them up? What a tragedy of immeasurable consequences—a mother who lost her mind and her soul. They will have to live with that. What about David, my poor husband, who sees that something is terribly wrong with me but can't fathom it? What will happen to the baby I am carrying, for whom I feel no emotional connection?"

## Reality versus Unreality

I tried to focus on verses of comfort from my Bible, with a ferocious intensity, but in so doing I became more and more obsessional. I turned all the Bible's encouragements against myself and applied all its condemnations to myself. Adding to my mental exhaustion, I scoured books that I thought might rescue me from these dark depths: books such as *Grace Abounding to the Chief of Sinners* by John Bunyan; *The Christian in Complete Armour* by William Gurnall; and *Spiritual Depression* by Martyn Lloyd-Jones. I gleaned some truth from these books that kept some hope alive, but it was all too intense and exhausting.

There were glimpses of reality but only occasionally and momentarily. Surely the Lord said, "I will never leave you nor forsake you" (Heb. 13:5). He stilled the storm for the disciples. He would never cast away any who truly seek him. What were the last twenty-five years of my Christian life all about? He never saves and then lets go. That was my daily debate.

Yet just as soon as I grabbed reality, delusional thoughts, subjective feelings, and deceitful unreality would crush all hope.

The beautiful sunshine and the singing of the spring birds were an agony. The beauty of the night sky and the array of stars, which testified of a faithful Creator, only served to break my heart yet further. I thought back to my childhood, when I would often sit outside my home in the Scottish Highlands looking heavenward and singing the words of Psalm 8:3–4:

> When I look up unto the heavens,
> which thine own fingers framed,
> Unto the moon, and to the stars,
> which were by thee ordained;
> Then say I, What is man, that he
> remembered is by thee?
> Or what the son of man, that thou
> so kind to him should'st be?[1]

But now, instead of that free and happy childhood, life was over. I had lost the Lord—if I ever had him. He was gone forever. All hope was gone.

## Spiritual Problem?

As a family doctor, I had treated many people in similar situations, and if I had heard my story in the consulting room, I would have objectively diagnosed: "Mentally broken and severely depressed." However, the subjective side of me— much more persuasive and persistent—convinced me that my problem was spiritual, a lack of spiritual will or trust. If only I could have greater faith in God, then everything would be okay. After all, "I can do all things through Christ who

---

1. From *The Psalms of David in Metre*, 1650.

strengthens me" (Phil. 4:13). But I was in the eye of the storm, weakened and disorientated, which is not the best place to make accurate assessments.

Eventually, when I finally crashed on the rocks in March 2003, David and I decided to call in my father, an experienced pastor of fifty years who would surely be able to find my spiritual problem. However, when he heard my story, he was convinced that it was not so much a spiritual problem as a mental and physical problem with spiritual consequences. He said that due to many factors, including burnout and long-term stress, my body was run-down and my mind was broken. The normal physical and mental processes were disrupted, and, as a result, the most precious thing in my life was profoundly affected—my relationship with the Lord. That was a massive turning point for David and me, and it led to God opening the door to a wonderful recovery and a beautiful refreshing of my life that I want to share with you in the rest of this book.

Although your story may not be as serious or severe as mine, my subsequent experience of meeting and counseling other women has convinced me that many Christian women are trying to do what almost destroyed me; that is, run overwhelming lives at an unsustainable and miserable pace. Although not all of you will end up crumpled on the ground, feeling close to death as I did, many of you are suffering somewhere on the spectrum:

stressed —> anxious —> overwhelmed —> burned out —> sad —> depressed —> suicidal

By God's grace my race did not end there, and yours need not either. Come with me to Refresh Gym and learn with me how to embrace a grace-paced life in a world of overwhelming demands.

## Refresh Gym

Usually when we visit a new gym, we want to immediately jump on all the fancy machines and get pumping. But the first station in Refresh Gym has no fitness equipment. Rather, it is a detailed personal examination to identify our weaknesses. In the past, I didn't appreciate how important this was.

When I moved from Scotland to the US ten years ago, I came across the fitness-fanatic phenomenon on an entirely different scale. Every American town and city seemed to boast multiple fitness wonderlands with lycra-clad, ear-budded ladies pumping the iron, sweating buckets, and downing shakes—not yummy milkshakes, but protein shakes. Gym names like Elite Fitness and Planet Fitness conjured up in my mind some surreal world where everyone was Jillian Michaels—superhealthy, superslim, superpretty, and never tired.

But David and I eventually succumbed to the marketing hype and signed up for two beautiful bodies. We had one brief complimentary session with a personal trainer, which amounted to little more than getting a photocopied sheet of identical exercises. No questions, no examination, no analysis of where we were weak or had particular problems. And off we went, pumping the iron and looking forward to big muscles (David) and losing a little weight (me) in just a few easy sessions. But nothing happened—not one muscle gained, not one pound lost. Pretty soon it fizzled out—apart from that nasty two-year contract.

Six years later we tried again, this time in a different gym, and this time it began with a detailed question-and-answer session and a test for injuries and weaknesses. David was even wired up to a computer that measured various physical factors and printed out a complicated bunch of graphs and tables to show him what he needed to work on. Recently, when I signed up my fourteen-year-old diabetic daughter, Joni, for an exercise program, the trainer spent the whole first session, and some of the second, just *talking*—asking multiple questions and making assessments—while everyone else in the gym was busy *doing*. I could see Joni's frustration, but I now understood how important this was to help identify problems and weaknesses, with a view to producing a fitness plan uniquely tailored to each individual's needs and for their maximum benefit.

That's why the first station in Refresh Gym is called "Reality Check"—it strips away our defenses and pretenses and makes us face up to reality. This examination will reveal our needs, highlight danger signs, help us identify problems and weaknesses, connect issues that we had not realized were related, and motivate us to tackle the other nine stations in the gym. So let's stop, get wired up to some diagnostics, and assess the damage our pace has been causing to various aspects of our lives. Not all of them will apply to you, but take note of the ones that do, and I'll tell you how to interpret them later.

### Examination

Many women find it helpful to actually write out or tick off these signs and symptoms. Not only can it be personally cathartic; it makes it more objective and gives a baseline for comparing changes for better or worse in the future. Another way to get the most out of the following checklist is to go through it with your husband or a close friend, as it can be difficult to accurately assess ourselves. As my friend Sarah explained:

> I have struggled off and on with depression/anxiety to varying degrees in my life, and in the darker times there was a part of me that *knew* objectively that it was what it was, but the lies in your head are so strong when the darkness is there, even if you can see it, you don't believe it.

## Physical Warning Signs

Just as running too fast round the track will eventually result in physical problems, so running the race of life at too fast a pace will have physical consequences. Over 70 percent of Americans experience stress-induced symptoms such as headaches, stomach cramps, sore joints, back pain, ulcers, breathlessness, bad skin, an irritable bowel, chest pain, and palpitations.[2] I certainly had some of these symptoms, and I also remember many female patients who came to me with multiple and varied bodily pains for which no physical explanation could be found, no matter how many tests and scans they had. Their lives were simply too fast and full for their bodies and minds. It's called "burnout" for a reason: all the stress causes chronic inflammation, a sort of fire in our cells that burns all the hotter, further, and longer the more fuel we add to it with our hectic lifestyles.

Feeling tired, exhausted, and lethargic all the time are early warning signs that should be heeded. Although sleep would seem to be the obvious cure, I found that I had difficulty

---

2. "Stress Statistics," Statistic Brain website, October 19, 2015, http://www.statistic brain.com/stress-statistics/.

getting to sleep. I woke up frequently. I was unable to get back
to sleep, and, therefore, no matter how many hours I spent in
bed, I was never rested or refreshed. Others may find that they
can do nothing but sleep. As one woman told me, "Generally,
when I'm stressed or anxious, I feel like I can't get enough
sleep. I think it can be both physical need and emotional—
as in, I'd rather stay in bed than face the day."

Weight gain through overeating, irregular eating, unhealthy eating, constant snacking, and lack of vigorous exercise should also concern us. For others it may be weight loss
through loss of appetite and skipping meals.

*Mental Warning Signs*

The next area to examine is our thought life. Remember
how difficult I found it to concentrate on anything? Maybe
you too are reading the same verses over and over during
your devotional time but struggling to remember what you
read. It's hard even to write your grocery list or prioritize
your to-do list. You end up just staring at your iPad or notebook. Or perhaps you have a plan, but you let yourself be
constantly sidetracked by interruptions and indecision and
never get to the store or to the first item on your to-do list.
The clinic appointment you wanted to change now has to
wait till tomorrow because the office is closed. The chicken
is still in the freezer, so it's Plan B for supper. You are late
again for that coffee date with your friend and having to
rush in the car. You can't decide what to do next—empty
the trash, make your bed, start supper, feed the dog, check
email, or go to the shop. You are forgetting things you used
to remember easily. Appointments, birthdays, anniversaries,
phone numbers, names, and deadlines are now slipping your

mind with scary regularity. You write your grocery list, then leave it at home. You spend endless hours second-guessing your choices and decisions.

Or perhaps, like me, you spend hours and hours obsessing about the same thing. It's like a repeating voicemail that you simply can't switch off. Most of your thoughts are negative. You dwell on the bad, the sad, and can't see the glad. Bad news, bad people, and always, "I'm a bad Christian." You are pessimistic about your church, your family, your job, and the nation. You are becoming hypercritical of yourself and others. One young mother told me her nightmare with obsessive thoughts:

> My family got sick right after our recent move. After that, I had obsessive thoughts about my children throwing up. I couldn't get it out of my head. *Was somebody about to throw up? What was that weird noise the baby made? Is he about to throw up?* I'd go in to get the kids after naps, half expecting to find them sick even though there was no reason to think that would be so. And I couldn't get the image out of my head. Multiple times a day I either pictured my children throwing up or a part of me expected them to start throwing up.

*Emotional Warning Signs*

Moving on to the emotions, you feel sad most of the time, often on the verge of tears, and sometimes cry for no obvious reason. Minor things make you cry. I remember crying in the car when another driver got into a parking spot before me when I was poised to get in there. I cried if the kids fought or acted foolishly, as I figured I was to blame. Laughter seems like a distant memory, faking it is becoming harder, and hearing others laugh is painful. Emotional numbness is the norm.

You wake with worry, live with worry, and go to sleep with worry. Your heart pounds and your stomach churns when you think of the day's decisions and people's expectations. You fear your children are going to turn away from God and end up in immoral and ungodly lives. The future looks hopeless, and you feel worthless. Maybe it would be better if you were not here, you think.

As if this emotional overload wasn't enough, we find ourselves taking on additional emotional burdens that God has not called us to carry. Stories of pain and need on social media and other media outlets capture our minds and our hearts, and every request for prayer seems to be addressed personally to us.

*Relational Warning Signs*

Frustration, irritability, and impatience are boiling inside you and often erupting. You're angry at your husband, your children, the pastor, the shop assistant, and that other driver.

Socializing is too much bother, and friendships are all in the past tense. You think about organizing babysitters and getting your house in order, but it's all too much hassle. Or you come home exhausted from work and would rather curl up in front of the TV or sleep than connect with any of your friends. Though you used to love interacting with people, you now avoid them because you haven't got the energy to talk or listen, and "they probably don't really like me anyway." You become increasingly isolated and lonely. As one of my friends said, "I felt lonely even when surrounded by people."

*Vocational Warning Signs*

You are overwhelmed in your calling. If you are a mother, you have little joy in your children and even wonder if they are worth all the effort. You feel trapped in an endless circuit of seemingly menial diaper changes, meals, lunches, dirty floors, crying kids, laundry, and generally being everybody's gofer. There is no clocking-off time, and you fall into bed at night exhausted, weary, with no sense of accomplishment, and dreading the next day. You hold yourself responsible for every accident, mess, crying fit, episode of bickering, and every failure of character in your children.

If you work outside the home, you're probably falling behind there too, feeling constantly overwhelmed. You are cutting corners and making more and more mistakes. Wrong decisions are easy and frequent. Indecision breeds procrastination, which breeds indecision. Instead of motivation and drive, there's apathy and passivity.

Despite all this, you find it difficult to say no, and you agree to every request that comes your way: school fundraising, making meals for needy families in the church, leading the women's Bible study, taking on nursery duty, driving your kids to multiple sports events, sitting on multiple committees, and saying yes to work that you know you can't possibly finish on time. You feel guilty or anxious when you are not running yourself ragged and consider yourself lazy if you take even five minutes to sit and have a break.

*Moral Warning Signs*

You are reading books and watching shows and movies with language and images you'd never have tolerated in the past.

You are fantasizing about close relationships with men to whom you are not married, or perhaps beginning to flirt with them at work or at church. You are shading the truth in conversations, exaggerating or editing as appropriate. You are medicating yourself (and your conscience) by overspending, overdrinking, overeating, or over-Facebooking. Most of your conversations are taken up with running down other people.

*Spiritual Warning Signs*

Are your personal devotions becoming shorter and shorter? Or are they nonexistent? Do you find yourself checking email and social media before your quiet time or even during it? Are you spending more time chatting with strangers on Facebook than time in conversation with God? Are you beginning to skip church for any reason you can think up? Are you finding church boring, sermons sleep-inducing, and Christian fellowship a drudge? Multiple yeses here should be ringing multiple alarm bells.

Another spiritual warning sign is gnawing discontentment. Lindsay, a young Christian, told me she has learned to be on the lookout for evidences of dissatisfaction in her life, often stemming from what she calls her "idealistic mind-set." "In a relationship," for example, "if things are not going the way I had imagined or wanted, I am often dissatisfied. This results in anxiety, a bad attitude, and ingratitude."

### Evaluation

That was a painful examination, wasn't it? But what does all the information add up to? Perhaps you got the all-clear, you're good to go and ready to run again. But if you're reading this book, it's more likely that you noted some worrying signs—probably many of them. What do you do now? The worst thing you can do is ignore these warnings and soldier on. Instead, you need to stop and take a serious look at them, evaluating them using three dimensions.

1. *How wide?* Given this broad range of symptoms, how many are you experiencing? Everybody will have some ticks—that's normal life in an abnormal world. But what should really get your attention is having more than half of them. Even if you have only a few, you should pay attention lest they multiply. In that case, you can use this book more as a preventative measure.

2. *How deep?* Try to gauge the seriousness of each tick by rating the intensity of each symptom from one to five, with five being the most serious. Obviously alarm bells should be ringing if more than a few are at three or four and above.

3. *How long?* We all go through down times; we have blue days or even a blue week. Again, that's just life in a fallen world. However, if these symptoms have been going on for a few weeks or more, then you really need to take urgent action and begin to address them.

So you've got your printout, and the measurements are concerning, the graphs are worrying, the evaluation is alarming. If you don't make adjustments to your life, you could move along the spectrum from stressed to anxious and overwhelmed, or even to sad, depressed, and ultimately suicidal. You are in real danger of crashing, and you must slow down. Refresh Gym is here to help you. Yes, some difficult decisions will have to be made if you sign up, but on the other side is a much better-paced and much more enjoyable life.

Or maybe you are tempted to despair. You shouldn't give

in to it. Just as God stopped me in my tracks to teach me some precious, lifelong lessons for which I will be eternally grateful, the fact that God has brought this book into your life and alerted you to the danger you are in should give you great hope. If he rescued me, he can rescue you, refresh your life, and get you back on track with greater physical, emotional, relational, moral, and spiritual health and with a good hope for a glorious finish.

As we move around the stations in Refresh Gym, remember that God owns the gym and is himself the trainer. His athletes are handpicked and very dear to him. His ultimate aim is to get you to the last station, Resurrection, which is not just an end-of-life experience; it can become a daily experience in your life. Yes, there is pain along the way, but God's tender, guiding hand will lead you through the process, and perhaps you will take others with you to this gym in the days ahead. "He knows the way that I take; when He has tested me, I shall come forth as gold" (Job 23:10). He's not just proving us but improving us.

# Replay

C

Growing up, I ran everywhere—and I always ran fast. The fact is, I couldn't just walk. Why walk when you can run? There was a life to be lived and a lot to cram into it. I ran to school and ran back from school. I ran to my friend's home and ran back to my home for supper. As a child, running was liberty. It felt good, it felt free, and tiredness was never an obstacle. Although the fields around my Scottish island home had numerous fences and gates, they were never obstacles to me. I just jumped over them. Why waste time opening them?

Then, in my mid-teens, I ran in a real cross-country race. There were two hundred kids, all kitted out in smart uniforms, all except my teammates and me—our small village school didn't have any. The gun fired, and I did what I always did. I just ran and ran, taking no notice of anyone else; up the hills, around the trees, looking only ahead until I was running alone. A few miles later, I had won my first real race without much effort. And so it continued in subsequent races.

I thought I would always win if I simply ran as fast as I could from start to finish.

That was until the standard got higher, the pressure got greater, and sheer willpower could not bring victory. In fact, when I moved up a level, it barely got me through the race. I was picked to compete in a race against experienced, well-trained runners who knew the game better than I did. But the course appeared straightforward, and soon I was sprinting. Running as fast as I could, I tore away from the group for the first half mile. At that point, to my dismay, the group behind me began to catch up. As they got closer and closer, my legs worked harder and harder. It was to no avail. Sufficient leg power was simply not there, no matter how hard I tried.

What was happening? I had never experienced this before. Reality hit my legs and willpower like a hailstorm on a sunny day. There was nothing I could do. The leaders tore past me, and I was unable to respond. My legs were heavy, my lungs were burning, and I struggled to keep going to the finish.

What went wrong? Obviously I ran too hard too soon and burned up all my reserves. My pace was fine for a short race but foolhardy in a long race against seasoned runners. My determined will was no match for them. To put it simply, I had a flawed race plan.

That painful experience damaged my ego as well as my budding athletic career, but the discomfort and distress soon passed. Little did I know that twenty years later I would experience another burnout that would be much more serious, long-term, and damaging, involving not just my body but my mind, my emotions, and my soul.

## Action Replay

The wise response to a badly run race is to watch an "action replay" and try to figure out what went wrong, and only then to attempt the next race. But some of us—myself included—have a natural inclination to put the past quickly behind us, forget the pain, get our running shoes back on, and return to the track as soon as possible. As another friend put it:

> Too much piled up, one thing after another, and I didn't stop to really deal with my stress or emotions. I just put my head down and kept going and going and going, which you can do for a little while, but you can't maintain that long term and not expect to see some damage. At some point you can't ignore the stress anymore and expect it to resolve on its own.

Refresh Gym does not allow this—thankfully. It forces us to stop, to look back, to replay the action, to face up to what went wrong, and to understand the causes of our stress, anxiety, and depression. Just as there are multiple factors that can adversely affect us in a race—our physical health, our food and drink intake, our sleep, our warm-up, and our footwear—so there can be multiple factors that adversely affect us in the race of life.

Before we take a look at that replay and identify these factors, though, let's dig a bit deeper and lay some biblical foundations that will help us understand the complex interaction of our bodies, our minds, and our souls. That will help us avoid taking simplistic body-only, mind-only, or soul-only approaches to our problems and their solutions. It will also grow our practice out of our theology, not only producing greater accuracy but also providing longer-term and deeper motivation than mere self-help advice.

## Practical Theology

Many practical problems are rooted in wrong theology. Other practical problems result from a failure to apply theology to our lives. That's where I went wrong in one particular area: applying the doctrine that God is our Creator. Throughout medical school, I was constantly taught the theory of evolution. Not once, though, did I entertain it as a valid theory. Not once did I doubt that God had created the world. However, looking back, I can see that I did not fully apply that doctrine to my life. There was a block between what I believed in my head and what I did in some parts of my life. Let me explain.

### We Are God's Creatures

The truth that God is our Creator is the first truth we find in Scripture, and it's placed first because it's so important. Remembering that God is our Creator and we are his creatures has many practical implications. It means that we are finite and dependent. It means that we must live in ways that respect that God has made us with limitations. But where do we find out about our limitations? We learn from God's Word the general truth that we are limited creatures. But we get the specifics of our limitations from God's world and personal observation.

By "God's world," I mean research findings that God has graciously enabled scientists to discover about how human beings function best. For example, a recent study from the National Institute on Aging found that exercise triggers brain cell growth and improves memory.[1] That got me moving! Information such as this is an expression of our Creator's love for us and should be read through the spectacles of Scripture to make sure it agrees with his Word. We'll do a lot of that in Refresh Gym. To live a grace-paced life, we need every grace-provided truth.

By "personal observation," I mean listening to our bodies and our minds, developing a sensitivity to when we are pushing ourselves beyond our limits. That's also God's gracious voice calling us to respect our creaturely limitations. He may also "speak" through family and friends who know us best and may express concern about our excessive working hours, lack of sleep, or poor diet.

## *We Are Complex and Limited Creatures*

We are not only creatures; we are complicated creatures. We have not only incredibly complex bodies but also remarkably intricate souls. And when you put these together in one person, you have multiplied complications as each part interacts with the other. That was one of the key areas I forgot. I was pushing myself physically in many different ways. God has blessed me with a strong will, and when I decided to get something done, I just kept on pushing until it was accomplished.

Yes, at times I could tell that such determined pushing was taking a toll on my body, but I failed to see that it was also taking a toll on my mind and my soul. I seemed to think that I could push and exhaust the physical part of me, and the mental, emotional, and spiritual parts would be unaffected.

---

1. "Running Releases Protein Associated with Improved Memory in Mice," *ScienceDaily*, June 23, 2016, https://www.sciencedaily.com/releases/2016/06/160623122940.htm.

I was not seeing myself as God had made me—a limited creature and a complex creature. I was not only underestimating my limitations but underestimating the impact of an exhausted body on my mind and my soul. And I'm not talking here about exceptional times in life when we have to push ourselves much harder, such as when facing exams, work deadlines, or nursing babies. I'm talking about this becoming the norm, the default, for extended periods of time. Verses such as Philippians 4:13—"I can do all things through Christ who strengthens me"—do not override our basic need to eat, drink, rest, and sleep.

*We Are Fallen Creatures*

Have you noticed that the more complicated your kitchen gadgets are, the harder they are to fix when they break? Some months ago, my spaceship of a washing machine broke and needed to be replaced. We had no hope of fixing it (believe me, we tried). It required a technician with a diagnostic computer and specialist tools, and the spare parts were ultraexpensive. Its complexity created additional problems when it failed.

Similarly with our humanity. Although God made us with perfect complexity, the entrance of sin into the world means we're now *fallen* complex creatures, and that creates even more problems. Sin has messed up every part of us—our physics, our chemistry, our biology, our structure, our plumbing, our minds, our emotions, our souls, and *especially* the way each part interacts with the others.

I suppose I knew all this in my head but I was not applying it to my life. These truths were not making a practical difference to the way I lived. Once I began to see the practical implications of being a limited, complex, and fallen creature,

I began to see God differently, I saw myself differently, and I saw my life differently. Instead of pushing myself further and further, faster and faster, I began to think much more consciously about my need to live dependently on my Creator and to respect the limitations he made as part of my design. I also began to understand and respond to the complex interaction between body, mind, and soul. Learning more about God as Creator, and applying it practically to my life, has been a massively stress-relieving truth. God as Creator is not just doctrine for apologetic debate but is of the most momentous practical value.

## How Did I Get Here?

When we understand our humanity, especially the interconnection and interaction of various parts of it, we are more likely to avoid simplistic and one-dimensional solutions to our problems. And with that background, we're now ready to look at some of the specific causes of our problems. When we replay our life race, what do we see that's damaged us along the way? Most causes can be divided into two main categories—our life situation and our lifestyle—although one often influences or even produces the other. So, how do we figure out what caused our damage?

Just as athletes need coaches to help them review their races, we can often benefit from a coach (e.g., our husband, a friend, or a pastor) to help us replay and objectively analyze our lives and so identify the causes of our problems. This will help us avoid the common extremes of either blaming ourselves for everything or blaming everyone else for all our problems. An honest friend can help us to see where we are responsible and where we are not. My friend Sophia, who has suffered with bipolar disorder, told me that although she has had numerous counselors over the years, her best counselor and coach is her husband. "He knows me best. He knows when I am depressed but also when I am maybe being lazy and need a little loving 'kick in the pants.'"

## Life Situation

Let's do an action replay of my life situation and then of my lifestyle choices to show you how this works. "Life situation" refers to things that we have little or no choice about or control over. Life happens. So, what did my life look like leading up to its crisis? What factors brought me to that point? On the face of it, everything looked fine. I was in my mid-thirties, happily married to David, a mother of two lively little boys (ages five and four) and a one-year-old girl, and I was expecting another. I had begun homeschooling my boys eight months before and also worked part-time as a family doctor. I lived close to my family, including my two elderly parents. Although life was busy—too busy, on reflection—David and I felt blessed in every way. Conscious of God's help and grace, I approached everything with enthusiasm and maximum effort, the way I had always done— sprint from start to finish.

### Challenges and Changes

But a number of things had been imperceptibly combining, which was gradually breaking me down. The first of these major events was a church split, which hugely impacted our family. For close to ten years (1990–2000), we had been in a terribly divided denomination that was failing to deal with serious moral issues. In the midst of this, in 1995, David had begun his ministry and was thrown into the ongoing controversy that was engulfing everybody. The atmosphere in our denomination was fearful and ominous. Much troubled water passed under the bridge. Eventually, after further years of stressful controversy, our denomination split in the year 2000, resulting in David and me being forced out of our beloved congregation. Many others among my family and friends were also deeply affected by this divide. Although the Lord felt close and provided for us in every way, these anxiety-filled days and years had been taking a deep though largely hidden toll.

Although I had to take on more medical work for a time, within a year of the church split and losing our congregation, God provided David with a new, large congregation to pastor in the Isle of Lewis. We moved to our new island home and into a new community, beginning all over again with new friendships, new responsibilities, new expectations, new colleagues, and, therefore, new anxieties. As a friend who moved to California told me, "Even when it's a good move and everything goes well, it doesn't mean the stress of all that newness isn't real."

Then came the marriage breakup of two Christian couples who were very close to me. Two dear friends left the faith. This rocked my sense of stability and security and left me reeling in confusion like the sailors of Psalm 107 or the disciples in the storm. I was beginning to feel overwhelmed. My life race was beginning to falter. On top of everything else, I was now also swirling in a sea of pregnancy hormones—probably the straw that broke the camel's back.

*Different Races*

No two races are the same. My life-race fail involved multiple changes on the one hand and multiple losses on the other—the loss of a denomination, of a congregation, of friends, of David's vocation (temporarily), and of our home. There was also the pain of long-term conflict, the pain of injustice, and the pain of my friends' marriage breakups and their spiritual backslidings. For Jeni, a pastor's wife, it began with the traumatic experience of being married, having a child with complications within a year, and not having the time to process that emotionally or to recover physically from the C-Section. Multiple children then followed in quick succession, all through C-section. Reflecting on this time, her husband, Greg, observed, "We did not give due appreciation to the toll that took on her body and the emotional stress of seminary years and the things that come with that. There was a neglect of health—nothing radical but just dietary—eat what you could afford, when you could, always running, little sleep, little relaxation."

In your case there may be other factors that you have no control over: illness, caregiving, financial loss, crime, disability, accidents, and so on. Another friend of mine crashed through a lot of changes in her life over a short period of time and even ended up in psychiatric care for a time.

It's quite common for women to tell me that they have no idea why they are so anxious, so sad, and so chronically tired. But when we start replaying the previous couple of years of their lives, they are often stunned to realize how many life changes and life challenges they have experienced. They are also relieved though, because there's something eye-opening and hope giving about understanding the connection between causes and effects. The absence of such identifiable connections adds to the perplexity and disorientation.

## Lifestyle

Now we want to move on to look at factors that we do have a choice about, things that we can largely control. For me, there was my long-term perfectionism. I had always had high expectations of myself, pushing myself to my limits in every area of life, even from a young age: in sports I was hypercompetitive; at med school I studied nonstop Monday to Saturday; at work I pushed through my residency year, working eighty-plus hours per week; in relationships I wanted to please everyone; in my spiritual life I wanted to be spent in the Lord's service and please the God I love.

My pace was getting faster and faster and faster with each passing year; no time to stop, no time to care for myself, and no limit to how much I could carry or cram into each day. I had only two gears—fast or very fast. Remember my childhood—why walk when you can run? I did not know any other way and had taken this pace into my adult life without knowing the dangerous consequences. This was a seriously flawed race plan.

I also had an excessive sense of responsibility for my children. Of course, I *was* responsible for them, especially in their youngest years. But I had taken full responsibility not just for what they ate and wore but for their behavior, their character, their educational success, and even their eternal destiny. I was constantly under a cloud of "mommy guilt" with my overactive conscience never letting my inner life have a moment of rest or peace. There was also a lot of pride in that I would rarely ask for help from David or others for fear of invading their space or giving the impression that I couldn't cope with it all. So on top of life conditions I had no control over, I had chosen to add perfectionism, people pleasing, false guilt, and self-sufficiency.

As with situational factors, the life choices that endanger you may be quite different from mine. Based on my counseling of others, the main dangers for women are:

- *Idolatry*. We make idols of beauty, fashion, career, husband, or children—especially their success in school and sports.

- *Materialism*. Our pursuit of money or bigger and better homes often results in working more hours or jobs than we can handle and also nourishes the worm of discontent that gnaws away at our minds and hearts.

- *Debt*. One of the greatest causes of stress is living beyond our means. Maybe we don't spend 50 percent more than we can afford, but 10 percent more, year on year, grows our debt and our anxiety levels.

- *Comparison*. Pinterest, Facebook, and mommy blogs can lead us to compare ourselves unfavorably with others who seem better looking, better homemakers, better organizers, and better everything.

- *Indiscipline*. Although it's hard to be disciplined and organized, it's more stressful to be the opposite, which so easily occurs as we use technology. How many hours are wasted on the Internet, resulting not only in guilt over wasted time but a pileup of other duties that now have to be rushed?

- *Identity*. We define who we are by our successes, our failures, or some part of our past, instead of who we are in Christ. We will discuss this in detail in a later chapter.

- *Unbelief*. If we believed that God cares for us even more than for the sparrows (Matt. 6:26), what angst we would escape and what peace we would enjoy!

- *Diet*. As we'll discover later in this book, there's a growing body of evidence that connects our moods and minds with our food. Eat junk food, and we'll have junk moods and minds.

- *Media diet*. Just as what we put in our mouths affects our emotions, thoughts, and hearts, so what we put in our ears and eyes has emotional, intellectual, and spiritual consequences. Many live as if Philippians 4:8 said, "Whatever things are false, whatever things are sordid, whatever things are wrong, whatever things are filthy, whatever things are ugly, whatever things are terrible, if there is any vice, and if there is anything worthy of criticism—meditate on these things."

- *Perfectionism*. We strive for flawless family, house, meals, and appearance. My young friend Linda, a student teacher, told me, "Perfectionism is what makes my burnout bomb tick. It is the most influential burnout factor in my life." She also remarked how it doesn't affect just one area of her life but shows itself in every aspect: her spiritual life, workplace, school, basketball, and relationships. "All these are affected by my desire to 'get it right,'" she said.

- *Failure*. We fail at school, or at a job, or at homemaking, or at parenting, or in witnessing, or we fail to meet our own or others' expectations. A college student explained to me how fear of failure can be so debilitating and depressing: "If it is flawed at all, it's worthless," she confessed; "I have a fear of failure, which leads to an attitude of avoidance. I will avoid something or a situation if I know I won't get it right."

- *Conscience*. Few things drain us like a guilty conscience. As the wise man said, "He who covers his sins will not prosper" (Prov. 28:13). But real guilt is not our only challenge. So many women I know experience false guilt. Satan is constantly harassing them with, "You are not doing enough."

- *Backsliding*. Is our devotional life shortening and shallowing? Do we rarely think about God or pray to him throughout the day? Are we slipping farther and farther away from him and closer to temptation and sin?

## Straws and Camels

That's a long list of life events and lifestyle issues, but it's not exhaustive. Use it as a sampler to replay and review your life. Don't ignore or minimize. It may not be one big issue but lots of smaller ones that can eventually break a person. We are all different with different vulnerabilities. Sometimes it truly is a straw that breaks a camel's back, but it's always the end result of years of mistreatment.

Remember also that damage in one area, perhaps the body, will usually impact us spiritually, emotionally, and intellectually. That's one reason we spent so much time earlier looking at how complex we are and how each part of us interacts with the others. In my personal experience, and in counseling others, one of the biggest breakthroughs on the way to healing comes when we take that holistic approach to causes and cures.

One last question that may have crossed your mind is, When do we know that we need a replay, that we need to stop and retrace our steps? My answer is that we should be regularly dropping in at the first station, Reality Check, for an assessment. If two or three of these warning signs are seen, we note them but are not overly worried. That's just life. But if five or more appear, or if even one of them is in the spiritual or moral category, then we should be making our way to the Replay station.

So what have we done so far? We have assessed the damage and understood the causes of it. We've begun to admit the harm we do when we live a space age–paced life rather than a grace-paced life. Let's now get on to the more practical and positive parts of this book as we walk over to the next station, Rest.

# Rest

By now, you're ready to start doing and get moving, but station 3 in Refresh Gym is full of beds. It's a strange gym, isn't it? At the first two stations we just talk, and at the third station we lie back and rest. Why?

When athletes finish a race or a particularly intense training session, they prioritize rest so that their bruised, tired, and injured muscles are given a chance to recover. Some athletes will even rest in an ice bath to minimize long-term muscle damage. We'll skip the ice bath, as I want to focus on the rest we derive from sleep, which not only limits and even heals damage from our life race but also helps us to run better and safer in the future. Sleep doesn't rest and refresh just our muscles, but our whole weary humanity. The lack of it can even be fatal, as Arianna Huffington, of *Huffington Post* fame, found out when she awoke one morning in a pool of blood.

Amid growing popularity and success, she had been depriving herself of increasing amounts of sleep. It dramatically caught up with her one morning when she collapsed with exhaustion and broke her cheekbone in a collision with her desk. In her best-selling book *Thrive*, she explains, "I was not living a successful life by any sane definition of success. I knew something had to radically change. I could not go on that way."[1] After focusing on improving her sleep habits, she's now become a vocal campaigner for increased sleep.

I've known many Christians over the years who have struggled with the consequences of sleep deprivation, myself included. That's why I want to add my voice to Huffington's by highlighting sleep as a vital component of recovery and future well-being.

## Sleepology

At this station, we'll be making appeals to scientific research to support the case for more sleep. One study highlighted that we are sleeping between one and two hours fewer per night than people did sixty years ago, and two and a half hours fewer than a hundred years ago.[2] However, ultimately the practice of getting a good night's sleep is rooted in the outworking of our theology. We believe God has made sleep an integral part of our humanity (Ps. 127:2), but as with all good gifts from God, we have a sinful tendency to refuse it or misuse it. While some may struggle with wanting too much sleep, many of us struggle with wanting to make do with too little. In our productivity-mad society, we idolize activity and minimize the need for sleep. We can even pride ourselves in how little sleep we seem to need. Stories of famous Christians throughout history who reported getting by on very little sleep fuel the idea

---

1. Arianna Huffington, *Thrive: The Third Metric to Redefining Success and Creating a Life of Well-Being, Wisdom, and Wonder* (New York: Harmony, 2015), 2.

2. James Gallagher, "The Arrogance of Ignoring Our Need for Sleep," *BBC.com*, May 12, 2014, http://www.bbc.com/news/health-27286872.

that less sleep is more godly and an example of great faith. What is often forgotten is that many of these Christians also suffered terribly ill health, and others died young. That's why I want to make the case that adequate sleep is a far better example of great faith. Think of all you are saying when you do take, say, eight hours of sleep each night:

> *I believe God will look after my family, my work, or my studies.* I refuse to believe the lie that everything depends on me. I believe in God's sovereignty and trust that he does not need me to overwork and undersleep to get all the work done (Ps. 127:1–2).

> *I believe God created my humanity,* and *I need to follow his guide for maintaining it.* I refuse to believe the lie that I'm unique. I'm no stronger than others and therefore equally in need of his gift of sleep (Pss. 3:5; 4:8). As Liberty University professor Karen Swallow Prior wrote: "Our need for rest is so central to our humanity that God set aside one day a week for it. In fact, one third of our lives is spent in sleep. . . . Indeed, rest is often treated less like friend and more like foe. We are never more vulnerable than when we sleep. Perhaps that's why we resist it so."[3]

> *I believe my body and soul are so closely bound together that each impacts the other.* I refuse to believe the lie that if I neglect my body, my soul and mind will still flourish.

> *I believe my sleep is one of the best illustrations of my rest in Christ.* I refuse to believe the lie that I must be known for my sacrificial service to Christ rather than by my resting on him.

---

3. Karen Swallow Prior, "Want to Follow God? Go to Sleep," *Christianity Today*, February 21, 2012, http://www.christianitytoday.com/women/2012/february/want-to-follow-god-go-to-sleep.html.

*I believe in God alone and refuse to worship idols.* I refuse to idolize work success and belittle sleep. I refuse to idolize late night entertainment and neglect sleep. I refuse to idolize service at the expense of sleep. I refuse to make impressing my boss more important than sleep. I refuse to idolize a perfect home at the cost of damaging the temple of my body. Our sleep patterns reveal our idols.

## Multiple Good Reasons to Sleep Longer

Before we discuss how to sleep better and longer, consider some of the devastating consequences of reduced sleep. Or, to put it more positively, following are multiple good reasons to sleep longer.

### Physical Consequences

Sleep prolongs and enhances life. To put it simply, without sleep we die; and with lack of sleep we may die much sooner. Numerous studies link the chronic lack of sleep (defined as less than six hours per night) with genetic damage, cardiovascular damage (such as hypertension and strokes), cancer, diabetes, infections, and inflammatory disorders such as rheumatoid arthritis. Chronic sleep deprivation is also associated with infertility and even obesity, with sleep loss triggering increased hunger and a desire for high-calorie foods. Far from sleep being a waste of time, it plays an essential role in the daily restoration of damaged body components and a major role in the prevention of disease.[4] It therefore gains us time in the long run.

---

4. Christine Gorman, "Why We Sleep," *Scientific American*, October 1, 2015, http://www.scientificamerican.com/article/sleep-why-we-sleep-video/. See also "How Sleep Can Help (or Hurt) Your Arthritis," NatraCure.com, http://natracure.com/blog/sleep.

*Sporting Consequences*

The physical consequences of too little sleep can be even better understood and appreciated when we examine sports science and learn why more and more elite athletes are increasing sleep and even hiring sleep coaches in order to improve performance. Research has found that two days of sleep reduction lead to a more than 20 percent reduction in attention span, reaction time, strength, stamina, accuracy, and speed. Little wonder that the average sleep time of top athletes is well above average.

Michelle Wie, the 2014 US Women's Open golf champion, slept for sixteen hours before the Sony Open. "When I can," she told *Golf Digest*, "I'll sleep more than 12 hours, and I don't feel good if I get less than 10." Prolific tennis champion Serena Williams said, "A lot of people underrate sleep. You need a certain amount of sleep to rejuvenate your body, to rejuvenate the cells and to perform, whether you're going to school or whether you're playing a professional sport. . . . When I don't get enough sleep I just can't get a good workout. It's low quality and I don't have enough rejuvenation in my cells to use the muscles that I need to use."[5]

*Intellectual Consequences*

"Yeah, but I'm no Serena Williams. I just sit at a computer all day, or taxi kids all day, or run around in circles all day in my home. I don't need to perform at such a high physical level."

5. Jessica Cumberbatch Anderson, "Serena Williams Tackles Insomnia as Co-Owner of 'Sleep Sheets' Sleep Aids," *Huffington Post*, April 4, 2012, http://www.huffington post.com/2012/04/30/serena-williams-tackles-sleep-problems-with-sheets_n_1465015 .html. See also *Sleep Disorders and Sleep Deprivation: An Unmet Public Health Problem* (Washington, DC: National Academies Press, 2006); "You Are What You Sleep," *Athlete Kinetics*, February 9, 2016, http://athletekinetics.com/2016/02/09/you-are-what -you-sleep/; and Jordan Schultz, "These Famous Athletes Rely on Sleep for Peak Performance," *Huffington Post*, August 13, 2014, http://www.huffingtonpost.com/2014/08/13 /these-famous-athletes-rely-on-sleep_n_5659345.html.

In *Sleep Is More Important than Food*, Tony Schwartz says the research is unanimous—the better you sleep, the more you learn: "Even small amounts of sleep deprivation take a significant toll on our health, our mood, our cognitive capacity and our productivity."[6]

Personally, I find that if I'm running low on sleep, my efficiency in managing my home drops significantly. I forget things, it takes me twice as long to get things done, I'm much less decisive, and I generally feel as if I'm in a fog. Even my kids notice it and will laughingly say, "Mom, you need a nap!" More seriously, I can't concentrate on my devotions without my mind flitting in a hundred different directions.

### Emotional Consequences

Although by sleeping less and working more the *quantity* of our work may increase in the short term, the *quality* definitely decreases, and so does our enjoyment in what we do. That's because sleep loss disrupts the brain's flow of epinephrine, dopamine, and serotonin, chemicals closely associated with mood and behavior. Thus, people with insomnia are ten times as likely to develop depression and seventeen times as likely to have significant anxiety. Studies led by Torbjörn Åkerstedt of Stockholm University found that less sleep reduces empathy levels but increases fear levels.[7]

I am in no doubt that lack of sleep played a significant role in the development of my own depression. Talking with others who have experienced burnout, I have found this to be

---

6. Tony Schwartz, "Sleep Is More Important than Food," *Harvard Business Review*, March 3, 2011, https://hbr.org/2011/03/sleep-is-more-important-than-f/. See also https://hbr.org/2006/10/sleep-deficit-the-performance-killer/ar/1#.

7. See a summary of Åkerstedt's research at Karolinska Institutet, Department of Clinical Neuroscience, http://ki.se/en/cns/torbjorn-akerstedts-research-group.

a consistent thread. It wasn't so much the occasional sleep-deprived night that pushed me over the edge. It was the repeated, habitual sleep deprivation that ultimately resulted in an overall run-down of health. I now notice very clearly that when my sleep hours go down, my mood and cognitive ability go down with them. This recognition is a key motivator for getting to bed on time.

### Social Consequences

Sleeping is a part of loving our neighbor, because lack of sleep damages those closest to us, especially our family and colleagues. It's not just that we become temperamentally fragile and impatient; we are also more likely to be involved in accidents. Do you ever notice how clumsy you feel after a bad night? Drowsy driving is as dangerous as drunk driving, with up to 100,000 auto accidents a year blamed on DWE, "driving while exhausted." Sleep is clearly a moral issue.

### Spiritual Consequences

But it's more than morality at stake; it's also our spirituality. Ponder this paragraph from Don Carson:

> If you are among those who become nasty, cynical, or even full of doubt when you are missing your sleep, you are morally obligated to try to get the sleep you need. We are whole, complicated beings; our physical existence is tied to our spiritual well-being, to our mental outlook, to our relationships with others, including our relationship with God. Sometimes the godliest thing you can do in the universe is get a good night's sleep—not pray all night, but sleep. I'm certainly not denying that there may be a

place for praying all night; I'm merely insisting that in the normal course of things, spiritual discipline obligates you to get the sleep your body needs.[8]

When lecturing about Charles Spurgeon's suffering with depression, John Piper said:

> I am emotionally less resilient when I lose sleep. There were early days when I would work without regard to sleep and feel energized and motivated. In the last seven or eight years my threshold for despondency is much lower. For me, adequate sleep is not a matter of staying healthy. It is a matter of staying in the ministry. It is irrational that my future should look bleaker when I get four or five hours sleep several nights in a row. But that is irrelevant. Those are the facts. And I must live within the limits of facts. I commend sufficient sleep to you, for the sake of your proper assessment of God and his promises.[9]

Did you notice how Piper connected time on the pillow with trust in God's promises? I believe part of my inability to hold on to God's Word in my worst days was caused by sheer exhaustion more than unbelief. I now agree with Karen Swallow Prior, who said that rest is paramount to a "successful" spiritual life. She describes herself as "fanatical about sleep" and goes on, "I used to think this refusal to burn the candle at both ends, even for the sake of church, work, or home, was selfish. Not anymore."[10]

8. D. A. Carson, *Scandalous: The Cross and Resurrection of Jesus* (Wheaton, IL: Crossway, 2010), 147.

9. John Piper, "Charles Spurgeon: Preaching through Adversity," Desiring God website, January 31, 1995, http://www.desiringgod.org/biographies/charles-spurgeon-preaching-through-adversity.

10. Prior, "Want to Follow God? Go to Sleep."

## *Women and Sleep*

Sleep is even more important and seemingly harder to come by for us women, as researchers at the University of Loughborough Sleep Research Center discovered. They found that "women need as much as 20 minutes more sleep than men each night in order to stave off hostility, psychological distress and depression."[11] It's not just that women's brains have more complex wiring than men's; women tend to multitask more, using up more of their brain reserves, and thus need more sleep to recover and repair.

Mothers of young children are especially sleep deprived when their children are waking up at night. On top of that, there's the constant multitasking all day long. And then some of us exacerbate the problem by staying up much later than we should, trying to get some quiet time. There are many extra challenges for women.

## A Few Sleeping Pills

By now, hopefully we realize that good sleep is a must. But how do we get there when there seem to be so many obstacles in the way? Here are a few helps to improve our sleeping habits and so receive God's good gift of sleep.

## *Knowledge*

If our schools substituted sleepology for algebra, our society would be a much healthier, safer, and brighter place. Despite sleep taking up a quarter to a third of our lives and having such an influence on the remainder, most of us leave school in

---

11. Janet Tiberian, "Researchers Recommend 20 Minutes More Sleep for Women," MDVIP, April 5, 2016, http://www.mdvip.com/community/blog/view/researchers -recommend-20-minutes-more-sleep-for-women.

total ignorance of the why and the how of sleep. As knowledge will not only guide us but also motivate us, why not follow up some of the footnotes in this chapter or read *The Power of Rest* by sleep doctor Matthew Edlund?[12]

### Discipline

Once we understand the physical, intellectual, emotional, social, and spiritual importance of sleep, the next challenge is to make it happen regularly. We need God's help to translate this conviction into action. Ask him for the willpower to make the necessary schedule adjustments and lifestyle changes (Phil. 2:13).

### Routine

Build routine and regularity into your sleeping and waking times. God made us with certain bodily rhythms and has so ordered it that the more we align with these rhythms, the more we flourish. You might have a few wakeful nights at first as your body adjusts to the changes, but you'll soon notice your body click with it, and going to sleep and getting up will become a lot easier.

### Media Fast

Earlier in the evening we need to switch off the TV, the technology, email, Facebook, Instagram, and movies and remove our devices from view, to another room. Let's help our brains climb into bed with the rest of our body, switched off and ready to sleep.

---

12. Matthew Edlund, *The Power of Rest: Why Sleep Alone Is Not Enough* (New York: HarperCollins, 2010).

## Family Cooperation

I'm a night owl, and David is a morning lark. Early in our marriage we established a healthy compromise, but now with five kids, ranging from twenty-one all the way down to four, life is much more complicated. Our older kids are both night owls and morning larks rolled into one, and like most young people they are still mastering their noise-reduction skills. Add to that the muscle-bulking protein shakes whizzing around in the blender at dusk and dawn, and the last-thing-at-night "forgot to do my homework" crisis. So, what do we do? We have the occasional family conference and come to a mutual arrangement which works for all of us. Some time ago, we established a 10:00 p.m. noise curfew Sunday to Thursday to ensure that everyone gets their needed sleep. We explain that it's part of doing to others what we would have them do to us (Matt. 7:12).

## Exercise

We all know that exercise is important for our physical health (1 Tim. 4:8). When our kids have a full day at the park or beach we say, "They'll sleep well tonight." Have you ever thought of applying this principle to your own sleep habits too? It may seem more obvious if you sit at a desk all day, but what if your job involves being on your feet all day? Is exercise still necessary? Yes, because even if we are working on our feet, we build up tension as we move from one task to the next to the next, trying to get everything done. On top of that are the inevitable frustrations we face in juggling multiple tasks or children. Some of us can spend hours in "fight or flight" mode with lots of adrenaline swirling around our system, but with no place for it go. This is damaging to our brain, emotions, and other parts of our body. Then bedtime comes, and we are still in that mode, unable to switch off the production of stimulating adrenaline. Nonwork-related exercise redirects all this nervous energy and gives it a physical outlet. This kind of exercise produces in us a healthy kind of tiredness that is conducive to sleep, not the mental tiredness that leaves us unable to sleep.

## Contentment

Few things foster contentment like a good night's sleep, and few things lead to insomnia more than discontentment. A life of relentless striving for money, stuff, position, or fame leaves a deep discontentment that eats away at sleep. Perhaps this is the main reason our society is so sleep deprived. When we seek our contentment in God alone, it is far more likely that we will experience deep and satisfying sleep (Ps. 37:4).

## Faith

On the occasional night that I can't get to sleep, the most common reason is anxiety about something, either about my family, my church, or my country (or, at the moment, trying to sell a house). These worries seem to shout very loud in the middle of the night. But so too can God's Word. In the silence of the night, when anxiety crawls into bed with me, it's a good time to exercise faith in bibical truth and let it wedge between anxiety and me. When I worry about my family, I believe God when he says: "But the very hairs of your head are all numbered. Do not fear therefore; you are of more value than many sparrows" (Matt. 10:30–31). When I worry about my lack of spiritual vitality, I believe him when he says: "If you then, being evil, know how to give good gifts to your children, how much more will your heavenly Father give the Holy Spirit to those who ask Him!" (Luke 11:13). When I worry about a perplexing providence and struggle to understand it, I believe him when he says: "Trust in the LORD with all your heart, and lean not on your own understanding. In all your ways acknowledge Him, and He shall direct your paths" (Prov. 3:5–6). When I worry about the future, I remember that God says: "I will never leave you nor forsake you" (Heb. 13:5).

These especially are the times in which we must remind ourselves that God is in total control. When we are able to sleep in these moments, we are resting securely in God's promises like the sleeping baby in his mother's arms.

### Accept Special Periods

There are times when, for exceptional reasons, we have to make do with less sleep. These times are usually short-lived and God-ordained, such as when mothers have babies, or when we are looking after a sick relative or having to be on call for work. God gives special sustaining grace at these times, but it's not supposed to be the norm or be prolonged. Such special seasons may require compensation in the short term, perhaps with a daytime nap. It is the long-term habitual pattern of sleep deprivation that leads to trouble.

### Napping

Many women, myself included, have found that a twenty- to thirty-minute daytime nap improves productivity, moods, and interpersonal relationships. Even some high-tech companies such as Google have set up nap pods or napping areas for staff. You may not always fall asleep, but the relaxation of a naptime can still be incredibly refreshing.

*Sleep Doctor*

But what if you've tried all these things and you're still exhausted through lack of sleep? It's not that you're neglecting sleep. No, you desperately want to sleep but can't. Perhaps the problem may have a physical component, such as the hormonal changes associated with menopause. It may be something such as sleep apnea.[13] Whatever it is, visiting a specialist, a sleep doctor, may be part of the solution. Use the multiple, legitimate God-given resources that are available to help you get to sleep.

## Sleep Theology

Ultimately, sleep, like everything else, should lead us to the gospel and the Savior. It prompts us to think about *death*, that we shall all close our eyes as in sleep and wake up in another world (1 Thess. 4:14). It teaches about our *Savior*. That Jesus slept (see Mark 4:38) is as profound as the fact that "Jesus wept" (John 11:35). It reminds us of Christ's full humanity, that the Son of God became so frail, so weak, so human, that he needed to sleep. What humility! What love! What an example! What a comfort! What a sleeping pill! It illustrates *salvation*. What are we doing when we sleep? Nothing. That's why Jesus used rest as an illustration of his salvation. "Come to Me, all you who labor and are heavy laden, and I will give

---

13. According to the Center for Disease Control, about 50–70 million U.S. adults have sleep or wakefulness disorder. "Insufficient Sleep Is a Public Health Problem," Centers for Disease Control and Prevention, September 3, 2015, http://www.cdc.gov/features/dssleep/.

you rest" (Matt. 11:28). It points us toward *heaven*. There remains a rest for the people of God (Heb. 4:9). That doesn't mean heaven is going to be one long lie-in. It means it will be a place of renewal, refreshment, comfort, and perfect peace.

I hope this helps you sleep more soundly—and have a sounder theology. No, you don't need to rest in an ice bath, but you do need to rest in order to recover your weary body and mind so that you can be ready for the next station in Refresh Gym—Re-create.

# Re-Create

C

Two years ago, I had surgery to repair my damaged hip joint and to remodel bone. After the initial resting on crutches, the next stage in recovery was the gradual reintroduction of exercise. This was not intense training but a gentle reconditioning and retraining of tendons and muscles. Too much too soon would cause damage rather than recovery of good leg function. Too little would leave the muscles weak and dysfunctional. Not until six months later was I allowed to throw caution to the wind and return to normal exercise. In this chapter we will try to find that wise balance between inactivity and overactivity as we pursue re-creation by recreation, especially by bodily exercise.

"Oh no!" you might think, "Another fitness fanatic who is going to tell me to run for miles, lift big dumbbells, drink weird protein shakes, and worse still—my biggest nightmare—wear Lycra yoga pants." Don't worry, if there's anything you'll learn in this book, it's to avoid idealistic extremes and find practical balance. But before we get to the more practical section, let's lay the foundation of a gospel-centered theology of the body. Because the way to begin and sustain regular physical exercise is not so much by monastic self-discipline or by the intense enthusiasm of some fitness instructors but by the inspiring and motivational truths of the gospel.

## Body Theology

Although the secular world has often emphasized the body to the exclusion of the soul, the church has sometimes veered to the opposite extreme of emphasizing the soul to the exclusion of the body. In some circles, any attempt to care for the body is viewed as unspiritual. A Christian lady once asked me, "Why do you go out running? Why don't you do something like knitting instead?" Running seemed kind of worldly to her, while knitting seemed more godly. If she had seen how poorly I knit, perhaps she would have changed her mind.

The Bible, however, finds the balanced path between these two extremes and guides us to care for both the body and the soul. The apostle Paul presents his theology of the body in 1 Corinthians 6:9–20. He starts by admitting that the human body has been damaged by sin (vv. 9–10). However, that doesn't mean we just forget the body. No, Paul says Christ's redemption is not just for the soul but also for the body. It's a full-body and a full-soul salvation. "The body is . . . for the Lord," insists Paul, "and the Lord for the body" (v. 13). He made it, saved it, and maintains an eternal interest in it.

More than that, your body is a member of Christ (vv. 15–17). It's not just our souls that are members of Christ; so are our bodies. That should have a huge effect on how we care for them. Think about that the next time you look in the mirror or stand on the scales.

And even more than that, your body is a temple of the Holy Spirit (v. 19). It's the Holy Spirit's house. He's taken up occupancy there. Think about how much you look after your own house. How much more should you look after the Holy Spirit's house?

And, if possible, there's an even greater motivation. Your body was bought with the price of Christ's blood (v. 20). He bought it with the greatest ransom ever paid. Try to think of the most expensive thing you ever bought. Was it a car or a house? How much did you protect it and maintain it? Now think of how much Christ paid for your body and consider how you are managing this blood-bought property. "You are not your own," says Paul. "You were bought at a price" (vv. 19–20). We have a new owner who has paid a huge price for his property. He claims our bodies as his own and calls us to manage them for his glory.

That's why his concluding appeal is "glorify God in your body" (v. 20). Paul's logic is simple. He bought you, body and soul. Therefore, serve him with body and soul. We will have to give an account to God for how we have used, abused, underused, or overused his property. That should make a difference not only to our view of our bodies but the way we manage them.

If that's a theology of the body, what does it mean in terms of practice? How do we glorify God with our bodies? That depends on whether we spend the majority of our lives sitting down at a desk job, or whether we spend our lives always on our feet.

## Stand Up

If our work involves a lot of sitting, part of the solution might be a stand-up desk, which enables us to work standing up, at least from time to time throughout the day. Researchers have discovered that we are sitting over nine hours every day, which is doing terrible things to our health, including increasing our risk of obesity, diabetes, cancer, and heart disease.[1] Many people, including my husband, David, have invested in a stand-up desk. These range from basic models to customized desks that zoom up and down at the push of a button. That's why my younger kids like to drop in at Daddy's office—to play with his desk. At home he devised his own stand-up desk using fifty dollars' worth of materials from Lowes. But we also need to have additional intentional exercise in our lives, whether we are homemakers or office workers.

## Intentional Exercise

I would define "intentional exercise" as that which is done exclusively for the benefit of our body, mind, and soul. In other words, such exercise is not incorporated into our work or intrinsic to our daily lives. "But hang on a minute!" you protest. "I spend all day every day on my feet—busy, busy, busy—then fall into bed at night exhausted. Are you seriously telling me I need to exercise?"

Yes, I am. All the research proves that adding exercise im-

---

1. P. T. Kazmarzyk, T. S. Church et al., "Sitting Time and Mortality from All Causes, Cardiovascular Disease, and Cancer," *Medicine and Science in Sports and Exercise* 41 (May 2009): 998–1005, National Center for Biotechnology Information, https://www.ncbi.nlm.nih.gov/pubmed/19346988. Olivia Judson, "Stand Up While You Read This," *New York Times*, February 23, 2010, http://opinionator.blogs.nytimes.com/2010/02/23/stand-up-while-you-read-this/. Neville Owen et al., "Too Much Sitting: The Population Health Science of Sedentary Behavior," *Exercise Sports Science Review* 38 (July 2010): 105–13, http://www.ncbi.nlm.nih.gov/pubmed/20577058.

proves life-work balance rather than damage it.[2] Let me il-
lustrate from my own experience. Prior to my burnout, my
life was a continuous whirl of driving kids around, in and out
of car seats, grocery stores, arranging appointments, paying
bills, phone calls, unexpected trips to the emergency room,
refereeing squabbles, lesson preparation, teaching lessons,
lesson corrections, nursing babies while toilet training toddlers, texts, responding to phone calls, emails, meal planning,
cleaning sticky floors and juice spills, and on and on. Or you
might say, on call 24/7/365. At work, this played out in the
stress of being a doctor on call through the night in a remote
Scottish island, never knowing if my next call was going to
be a cough or a road accident with fatalities. Yes, there was a
lot of running around. In fact, I thrived on it, or so I thought.
But way too much of my busyness was mental, not physical. The result? Classic stress. A constant swirl of adrenaline
rushing around my body that my incidental physical activity
could never sufficiently expel, and the outcome was mental
and emotional damage. Do you see yourself in this? Are you
constantly on the run but not actually running? I had long
forgotten my running days and was much too busy to inten-
tionally exercise. Then payback came with a very big crash.

*Intentional Exercise and Your Brain*

Moderate physical exercise helps to expel unhelpful chemicals from our system and stimulates the production of helpful
chemicals. It not only strengthens the body; it also strengthens
the brain. Research has shown that walking just two miles

---

2. Russell Clayton, "Want a Better Work-Life Balance? Exercise, Study Finds," *Science Daily*, January 9, 2014, https://www.sciencedaily.com/releases/2014/01/140109101742.htm.

a day reduces the risk of cognitive decline and dementia by 60 percent and increases problem-solving abilities and efficiency. And it's not just long-term benefits; exercise triggers the growth of new brain cells in the hippocampus and the release of neurotrophic growth factors—a kind of brain fertilizer that helps the brain grow, maintain new connections, and stay healthy.[3] Exercise and proper rest patterns generate about a 20 percent energy increase in an average day,[4] while exercising three to five times a week is about as effective as antidepressants for mild to moderate depression.[5] It lowers stress and anxiety levels and increases problem-solving abilities.[6]

But why do we need this when our mothers never knew what Lycra was? A recent study by *Prima* magazine compared calorie intake and calorie burn of 1950s women and modern women and clarified what I think we all probably suspect, that "the housework and general exercise that stay-at-home housewives did in 1953 was more successful at shedding the pounds," burning in excess of one thousand calories a day through their busy and heavy domestic duties, whereas today the female average is only 556 calories. They walked to

3. Norman Doidge, "Our Amazingly Plastic Brains," *Wall Street Journal*, February 6, 2015, http://www.wsj.com/articles/our-amazingly-plastic-brains-1423262095. See also "How Stress Affects Your Brain," Ted Ed.com, February 20, 2015, http://ed.ted .com/lessons/how-stress-affects-your-brain-madhumita-murgia. Nicole Spartano et al., "Midlife Exercise Blood Pressure, Heart Rate, and Fitness Relate to Brain Volume 2 Decades Later," *Neurology*, Neurology.org, February 10, 2016, http://www.neurology .org/content/early/2016/02/10/WNL.0000000000002415.

4. Sam Fahmy, "Low-Intensity Exercise Reduces Fatigue Symptoms by 65 Percent, Study Finds," *UGA Today*, February 28, 2008, http://news.uga.edu/releases/article/low -intensity-exercise-reduces-fatigue-symptoms-by-65-percent-study-finds.

5. M. Babyak et al., "Exercise Treatment for Major Depression: Maintenance of Therapeutic Benefit at 10 Months" *Journal of Psychosomatic Medicine* 62 (Sept–Oct 2000): 633–38, http://www.ncbi.nlm.nih.gov/pubmed/11020092. Andrea Dunn et al., "Exercise Treatment for Depression," *American Journal of Preventative Medicine* 28 (January 2005): 1–8, http://www.ajpmonline.org/article/S0749-3797(04)00241-7/ abstract.

6. Kirsten Weir, "The Exercise Effect," American Psychological Association, http:// www.apa.org/monitor/2011/12/exercise.aspx.

the shops, whereas we drive; they walked the kids to school, whereas we now have buses and vans; and we have washing machines and dishwashers, whereas they did most of the washing by hand; they walked to speak to colleagues at work, whereas we email and instant-message them.

But it's not just that we burn fewer calories; we also consume a lot more: 2,178 a day now as opposed to 1,818 then. This is mainly because they ate more fresh food than we do. *Prima* editor Marie Fahey commented: "It is telling that modern technology has made us two-thirds less active than we were. It goes to show the importance of exercise in the battle to maintain a healthy balance."[7]

Okay, so that looks like a very worrying trend. How do we women incorporate healthy exercise into our lifestyles? The good news is that we don't need to sell our dishwasher or washing machine—these are blessings from God. But we do need to add intentional exercise to our lives, and I want to give you a template for it.

### Prioritize Exercise

If you are married, and especially if you have kids, then any exercise program has to involve the cooperation of your husband. Make it a family priority, not just for you but also for your husband and kids. For years David and I did not make this a priority for ourselves, despite the fact that sport had been such a major part of our lives when we were young. The truth is, we both thought that natural fitness from our youth

---

7. See "How 1950s Women Stayed Slim," *Daily Mail*, http://www.dailymail.co.uk /health/article-191200/How-1950s-women-stayed-slim.html#ixzz4DARvkRgk. Also Celia Hall, "How 1950s Wives Kept Fit on a Diet of Hard Work," *Telegraph*, August 5, 2003, http://www.telegraph.co.uk/news/uknews/1438033/How-1950s-wives-kept-fit -on-a-diet-of-hard-work.html.

would carry us through life. That was until David developed pulmonary emboli (blood clots in his lungs) and hernias in his mid-forties. My burnout had been ten years earlier. But now we both understand, loud and clear, that exercise must be prioritized if we are ever to maintain the physical and mental fitness to serve the Lord for many years to come.

Women in employment also face the challenge of fitting in exercise after an exhausting working day. My friend Kay, an accountant, exercises early in the morning before work. Others use their lunch hour. Younger women often find it helpful to take part in college sports or in a recreational sports league, where the combination of exercise with social interaction is a great motivator.

## Challenges to Exercise

Several things can get in the way of exercising regularly. Back on the Scottish island where we previously lived, the weather made outdoor exercise difficult in the winter. Cold, driving winds and horizontal rain made walking or running a miserable experience. Michigan winters also make both walking and running difficult. For you, it may be that you live in a busy city with no place to walk or run away from the constant din of traffic. For others it may be that your husband can't get home from work till late, too late for you to exercise and refresh.

In response to these challenges, many women have tried to set up a small home gym, which works well for some. I found it hard to exercise at home due to the boredom factor of running on a treadmill and too many interruptions from children, and I was stressed out trying to make supper in between short bursts on the treadmill. Judging by the number of bikes, treadmills, abdomasters, weights, and other fitness paraphernalia I see on craigslist or at garage sales, I suspect many other women have the same problem.

Another challenge is the preconceived notion that only one exercise works for you. I had always considered running to be the best exercise for me. Thankfully, I came to realize that there is a world of other options. Perhaps you live alone but don't want to exercise alone. Meet up with a friend to exercise, join a gym, or maybe even get a dog—one that needs walking every day. Company definitely helps.

*Plan Exercise*

With exercise, I've come to realize that unless it's on my calendar, it's not going to happen. I have two group fitness sessions on my weekly schedule, and at the beginning of each week I get with David and my kids to make sure our schedules don't clash. If something does come up, then I pull out the YMCA schedule and find another slot that works. Wherever you exercise—at a gym, in your community, or in your basement—the time has to be carved out in advance and protected. If you plan to exercise while you have young kids who need to be watched, figure out a time when your husband can watch them, or put them in the gym nursery as I do. That uninterrupted exercise time has a twofold benefit: physical refreshment and mental renewal, re-creation through recreation. As Sarah said to me of her simple gym routine, "The uninterrupted time is almost as good as the exercise itself."

*Get Advice*

If you are really out of shape, you should see your doctor before beginning any kind of exercise program. David asked the advice of one of his students, who happened to be a trainer at our local YMCA. Through him, we took out a family membership there and began a family journey that we have come to love. We discovered a huge variety of classes, equipment, swimming options, running options, and a special area, called the Kid Zone, for children. Staff and trainers are refreshingly enthusiastic and are always willing to guide and instruct on how to best use the equipment and achieve our aims.

The wonderful thing about our local YMCA is that it is also one of the city's main rehabilitation centers for the physically challenged. Alongside able-bodied people are wounded vets, some with mechanical legs; elderly stroke victims; and kids with cerebral palsy.

It's a place of wonderful diversity: skinny people and round people, weak guys and muscle men, teenagers, middle-agers and seniors, all with the aim of improving their fitness. It is not unusual to see people from each of these groups making their way around the running track at the same time. Thus the whole experience is refreshing, motivational, and inspirational. There is room for everybody. How this reminds me of the church of Christ and its diversity! I leave that place feeling refreshed and ready for the next challenge.

### Have a Clear Aim

The key to exercising regularly is not so much *what* we do but *why* we do it. It's vital to have a clear aim to motivate you. That might be losing weight, building strength, increasing stamina, or simply relaxing. For me, it was stamina and muscle tone (after my body had taken a battering from five pregnancies) and mental and emotional refreshment.

## Build Slowly

Be realistic. Know your aim and gradually build up to it, be it to walk five miles, run five miles, lift fifty pounds, or whatever. Start with a much shorter distance or lighter weights. That way, you won't get hurt, and you will enjoy it. This is where a class is very helpful. There you see others at different stages of reaching their targets, and you pick up a lot of tips on what is appropriate, safe, and achievable. When I found a fitness class that suited my aims, I initially attempted to keep up with the other attendees, many of whom were lifting heavy weights. By the end of the class I was buckling and wobbling like jelly. My type A personality got the better of me. If I had been sensible and a whole lot humbler, I would have copied the ladies using lighter weights. The second time around, I ate humble pie. Two years later I can handle some heavier iron and am a lot stronger. So start slow and, if need be, swallow your pride. It took me a year before I had the nerve to buy myself Lycra yoga pants.

## Have a Weekly Routine

Given the power of habit, it's easier to do something regularly and routinely rather than just when we feel like it or can fit it in. I go to the same group-fitness class twice a week. It involves exercising all the major muscle groups, doing reps, and expending a lot of energy. I enjoy it so much that I would go every day if I could, but I need balance, not extremes. Occasionally I fit in another session. During my class my teenage kids often swim or do their own workout, and my little boy loves an hour at his play class in the Kid Zone.

## Play

It is so important to enjoy whatever exercise we do. If we just grind out the miles, reps, sets, and classes, exercising becomes just another round of performance targets as it morphs from a grace to be received into a law to be obeyed. All the pleasure and benefit are drained away, and eventually we will give it up.

Vary it. Vary your classes. Vary the exercise you choose to do as the seasons change. Little can beat exercising in the outdoors on beautiful, sun-kissed days. Play outside with your kids in the yard or pool. Regular exercise makes you fit enough to enjoy these fun sessions.

## Be Accountable

Keeping a record of your daily exercise can also form the basis of accountability with your husband, a trainer, or a friend. It is also fun to chat with your family and friends about what you each enjoyed while exercising that day. You are building refreshing and re-creating habits for life for all of you. There is currently a billboard advertisement by our local highway that shows a picture of kids exercising and contains this slogan:

> They learn from watching you—
> Be more active and your kids will too!

But now, after all that exercise, you'll be glad to know that we're going to relax. Yes, we need to get our bodies moving again, but we also need to learn how and when to unwind, both physically and mentally. Living a grace-paced life receives the grace of sweating but also the grace of chilling.

# Relax

Ever since my first child was born, my mother has on occasions said to me, "Shona, be good to yourself!" Now, you may think that sounds like very unbiblical advice. Does she want me to become selfish? In fact, it sounds even stranger coming from my mother, whose whole life has been defined by godly service and self-sacrifice. From as far back as I can remember, she worked tirelessly in God's strength from morning till night, caring for our family and serving God's people at every opportunity. But she also had two other practices that I believe have preserved her until now in her eighty-ninth year. She napped, and she watched the news. In fact, she still does. No matter how busy she is, she knows when to stop for a few minutes or longer and refuel with a short nap and a brief dose of politics, which has always fascinated her.

That's why, whenever she saw me frantically running from one responsibility to another to another (which was often), she would caution me, "Shona, be good to yourself!" In other words, "Stop what you are doing, take a break, and refresh."

That's why this station in Refresh Gym is entitled "Relax" and calls us away from our frantic lifestyles.

## Ms. Frantic or Ms. Reflective?

Perhaps you've met Ms. Frantic. She arrives at the gym at 8:00 a.m. Hours later, she's still pounding the treadmill, pumping iron, and powering away on the rowing machine, barely stopping to catch snatched sips from her water bottle. She looks exhausted, miserable, and ready to faint, but still she goes on. You ask her why she is doing this, and she replies, "Because I must." When you press her, asking, "But, why must you?" she looks at you strangely, and impatiently exclaims, "I don't know, I just must! There's always more to do."

Ms. Reflective also starts bright and early at 8:00 a.m., but she's different. She uses the same machines and works equally hard at points, but not all the time. Every now and then, she enjoys a drink of refreshing cold water. Sometimes she pauses to look out the windows and simply watch the world go by. She laughs at the children splashing in the nearby swimming pool. She even spots a friend exercising and has time to wave, give a big encouraging smile, and sometimes chat. Now ask yourself, "Which of these two images reflects how I live my life before God?" Am I Ms. Frantic or Ms. Reflective? Am I overworking and over-stressed, or am I taking time to think and to enjoy God's world?

## A Martha World

"Women Are Working Themselves to Death," warned a recent headline.[1] It was based on a joint study by Ohio State Univer-

---

1. Jessica Mattern, "Women Are Working Themselves to Death, Study Shows," *Woman's Day*, July 5, 2016, http://www.womansday.com/health-fitness/news/a55529/working-women-health-risks/.

sity and Mayo Clinic that compared almost eight thousand men and women over a thirty-two-year period and found that working over forty hours a week did serious damage to women's health, causing increased risk of heart disease, cancer, arthritis, and diabetes.[2] Working sixty or more hours a week *tripled* the risk of these conditions. Not surprisingly, the report's lead author, professor Allard Dembe, warned: "People don't think that much about how their early work experiences affect them down the road. . . . Women in their 20s, 30s, and 40s are setting themselves up for problems later in life." Unexpectedly, the risks are elevated only for women, not for men. Further analysis led the researchers to conclude that the greater risk to women is not necessarily because women are weaker but because they are doing so much more than men:

> In addition to working at a job, women often come home to a "second shift" of work where they are responsible for childcare, chores, housework, and more, according to sociologists. All of this labor at home and at work, plus all the stress that comes along with it, is severely affecting women. Research indicates women generally assume greater family responsibilities and thus may be more likely to experience overload compared to men.[3]

Professor Dembe also pointed to less job satisfaction among women because they have to juggle so many obligations at home as well. But this is not a problem just in the greater culture; it's a problem in the Christian population too. A survey of over a thousand Christian women, sponsored by *Christian*

2. Misti Crane, "Women's Long Work Hours Linked to Alarming Increases in Cancer, Heart Disease," Ohio State University, June 16, 2016, https://news.osu.edu/news/2016/06/16/overtime-women/.

3. Mattern, "Women Are Working Themselves to Death, Study Shows."

*Woman* magazine, found that 60 percent of Christian women work full-time outside the home. Reflecting on this, Joanna Weaver, author of *Having a Mary Heart in a Martha World*, commented, "Add housework and errands to a forty-hour-a-week career, and you have a recipe for weariness." But she also warned homemakers: "Women who choose to stay at home find their lives just as full. Chasing toddlers, carpooling to soccer, volunteering at school, baby-sitting the neighbour's kids— life seems hectic at every level."[4] Maybe you're now seeing Ms. Frantic in the mirror or hearing her in your heart and mind.

## Our Inner Orchestra

Every Christian wants to know God more; few Christians fight for the silence required to know him. Instead, we spend our days smashing stillness-shattering, knowledge-destroying cymbals on our ears and in our souls. And with so many gongs and clashes in our lives, it can sometimes be difficult to isolate and identify them. So let me help you do this and then provide some mufflers.[5]

First there's the din of guilt, the shame and embarrassment of our dark moral secrets: "I should have . . . I shouldn't have . . . I should have . . . I shouldn't have . . . " clangs noisily in our deep recesses, shattering our peace and disturbing our tranquility.

Then greed starts banging away in our hearts with its relentless drumstick: "I want it. I need it. I must have it. I will have it. I got it. I want it. I need it." And so on.

And what's that angry metal beat? It's hate stirring up mal-

---

4. Joanna Weaver, *Having a Mary Heart in a Martha World* (Colorado Springs, CO: Waterbrook, 2000), 7.

5. Part of this section was previously published in *Tabletalk*, the monthly magazine of Ligonier Ministries. Used by permission.

ice, ill will, resentment, and revenge: "How could she . . . I'll get him! She'll pay for this!" Of course, anger often clatters into the cymbal of controversy, sparking disagreements, debates, disputes, and divisions.

Vanity also adds its proud and haughty thud, drowning out all who compete with our beauty, our talents, and our status. "Me up . . . him down, me up . . . her down, me up . . . all down."

Anxiety tinkles distractingly in the background too, rapidly surveying the past, the present, and the future for things to worry about: "What if . . . What if . . . What if . . . " And is that the little, silver triangle of self-pity I hear? "Why me? Why me? Why me?"

The repetitive and unstoppable jangle of expectation comes from all directions—family, friends, employer, church, and especially from ourselves. Oh, for even a few seconds of respite from the tyranny of other people's demands and especially from our demanding, oversensitive conscience.

And smashing into our lives wherever we turn, we collide with the giant cymbals of the media and technology: local and international, paper and pixels, sound and image, audio and video, beep and tweet, notifications and reminders, and on and on it goes.

Is it any wonder that we sometimes feel as if we're going mad? Clanking and clanging, jingling and jangling, smashing and crashing, grating and grinding. A large, jarring orchestra of peace-disturbing, soul-dismantling cymbals. Then.

"Be still and know that I am God."

But how?

## Silencing the Cymbals

We can silence the cymbal of guilt by taking faith to the blood of Christ and saying, "Believe!" Believe that all your sins are paid for and pardoned. There's absolutely no reason to have even one whisper of guilt. Look at that blood until you grasp how precious and effective it is. It can make you whiter than snow and make your conscience quieter than the morning dew.

Greed is not easily silenced. Maybe muffled is about the best we can expect. Practice doing with less than usual, practice not buying even when you can afford it, practice buying nothing but necessities for a time, and practice spending time in the shadow of Calvary. How much less you'll find you need when you see how much he gave! Draw up your budget at the cross (2 Cor. 8:9).

Our unholy anger can be dialed down by God's holy anger. When we feel God's hot rage against all sin and all injustice, we begin to chill and calm. Vengeance is God's; he will repay.

The doctrine of total depravity is the ultimate dampener of personal vanity. When I see myself as God sees me, my heart, my mind, and even my posture change. I stop competing for top spot and start accepting the lowest place. "He must increase, but I must decrease" (John 3:30).

Hey! I'm beginning to hear some quiet now. But there's still that rankling anxiety tinkling away. Oh, to be free of that!

Fatherhood.

What?

Yes, the fatherhood of God can turn the volume of anxiety to zero. He knows, he cares, and he will provide for your needs. Mute your "what-ifs" at the bird feeder (Matt. 6:25–34). As mother-of-two Sarah told me, "Sometimes the things that can start to burn you out or cause you weariness are often things you can't leave. Just because you're feeling burned out by the responsibilities surrounding your husband and kids doesn't mean you can just up and leave—sometimes not even just for an afternoon! Sometimes you just have to put your head down and persist—but at the same time it is important to take to our Father in heaven our emotions and weakness and weariness."

Oh, and call in total depravity again when self-pity starts up. "Why me?" cannot stand long before "Why not me?"

"She has done what she could" (Mark 14:8). Don't you just love Christ's words to Mary when she anointed his head? What an expectation killer! Every time the despotic Devil, other people, or your tyrannical conscience demands more than you can give, remind them of Jesus's calming words, "She has done what she could."

Isn't that growing silence silver? But it can become golden if you go the extra mile and deal with the noisy intruders of media and technology. And that's where I want us to focus next.

### Daily Refreshment

We've all seen how marathon or triathlon courses have multiple refreshment stops along the way. Without these, runners would collapse with dehydration and exhaustion. I want to help you build some refreshment stops into your life, with the intent of slowing you down and quieting your heart and mind. First, we'll visit some small *daily* stops; then we'll visit a bigger *weekly* stop before concluding with an *annual* stop.

## The Digital Deluge

Digital technology is killing us. It's killing our souls and our bodies. It's killing our marriages, families, and friendships. It's killing our listening skills and speaking abilities. It's killing face-to-face communication and interfamily relationships. It's killing our minds, especially our ability to focus and concentrate. It's killing communion with God as it usurps communication with him first thing in the morning and last thing at night. It's killing our peace with its never-ending blizzard of notifications, beeps, and buzzes. It's killing our mealtimes through constant interruptions and distractions. It's killing God's voice throughout the day as we fill every traffic and bathroom stop with social media check-ins. It's killing our morality as the tsunami of porn drowns multitudes of young and old, male and female. It's killing our health, especially through its shortening, shallowing, and interrupting of sleep. It's killing our beauty intake as we walk through the spectacular with our heads buried in the black hole of our devices. It's killing our education as social media distracts and diverts students in classrooms, lecture halls, and libraries. It's killing our finances as productive work time is stolen from our employers to be frittered away on triviality. It's killing the service of others as we selfie ourselves into self-obsession. It's killing our identities as we cultivate and project so many social media personas that we've forgotten who we really are. It's killing privacy as every moment is now digitized not for family archives but for instant upload to the world for likes and hearts by complete strangers. Digital technology has punctured every part of our being and is draining the life out of us.

Want to restore some sanity? I've found three helpful ways

to calm my use of digital technology, build quiet into my days, and renew my inner life. I can't say I do all these perfectly, but these are my ideals.

1. *Mute phone and computer notifications.* We've become beep-and-ping-aholics. Turning off these notifications breaks the addiction element but also gives the mind time and space to relax or to concentrate on tasks without constant distractions and interruptions.

2. *Limit check-ins.* The average person checks her phone nine times an hour, and 110 times a day, with peak hours being between 5:00 p.m. and 8:00 p.m. Kleiner Perkins Caufield and Byers's annual Internet Trends report for 2013 found the average user checks the phone nearer to 150 times per day.[6] If each check-in takes only a minute (and it's usually far more), that's two to three hours a day lost to productivity or relaxing. According to the Pew Research Center, women spend an average of twelve hours per week using social media—that's nearly two hours a day![7] One of my friends was startled when I told her this, but after thinking about it, she admitted, "I can see how this is true! It doesn't seem like so much because it's just a few minutes here and a few minutes there, but they add up."

In my crusade for peace and quiet, I check email only three to four times a day and social media once a day. Unless something is really urgent, I don't reply immediately—same goes for texts and voicemail. I try to respond to everything during the one time each day I set aside for administrative tasks. I

---

6. Mary Meeker and Liang Wu, "Internet Trend Conference 2013," *Kleiner Perkins Caufield and Byers*, May 2013, http://www.kpcb.com/blog/2013-internet-trends.

7. Veronica Jarski, "The Women of Social Media: Digital Influencer Study," *MarketingProfs*, April 20, 2013, http://www.marketingprofs.com/chirp/2013/10575/women-of-social-media-digital-influencer-study.

don't carry my phone around with me at home. Instead, I store it somewhere out of reach, reducing the likelihood of checking it compulsively. Limiting check-ins also ensures I am present in mind as well as body with my kids and my husband. Out in the yard, I do the same. Phones are banned from the table at our mealtimes and during family devotions. Although there are some exceptional circumstances where some people's family situation or job description might necessitate increased phone connection, most of us can easily and significantly reduce our phone dependence.

3. *Meet with God first.* When I start my day with email, social media, or the news, my subsequent Bible reading and prayers are a distracted mess. I prefer to get a cup of tea, enjoy the silence, and meet with God first. Then I can start my day in a calm frame of mind. It makes the day more conducive to being caught up with God than with everyone and everything else out there. It also gives my mind a much-needed rest.

As I said, these are my ideals. I can't say I always succeed in meeting them, but when I do, I enjoy much more peace and productivity. I'm always looking for new ways to reduce digital stimulation and increase mental calm, such as not checking the phone when I'm standing in line or using the "Do not disturb" feature. Experiments on mice found that two hours of daily silence produced new brain cells in the hippocampus, the area of the brain associated with learning, memory, and emotion.[8] If it did that for mice, what could it do for you?

---

8. Imke Kirste et al., "Is Silence Golden? Effects of Auditory Stimuli and Their Absence on Adult Hippocampal Neurogenesis," *Research Gate*, December 1, 2013, https://www.researchgate.net/publication/259110014_Is_silence_golden_Effects_of_auditory_stimuli_and_their_absence_on_adult_hippocampal_neurogenesis.

*The She Shed*

Maybe you've heard about the "she shed" craze. It's basically a little hut in the yard reserved just for one person. Usually painted with pretty colors, and surrounded by a little garden of flowers and shrubs, it's a place for you to retreat and get some undisturbed time away from everyone else. In a recent video on she sheds, psychologist Jane Greer commented, "When you're depleted by giving to your family, to your partner, to everyone and everything around you, you need to be able to give to yourself, and this is a great way to do it."[9]

But there's no need to head off to the DIY store. You don't need a she shed to have a she hour. One of the first things I try to do when counseling women with depression is to have them schedule an hour in the day when they stop what they are doing, find a quiet spot, and read a book or do something creative. Women with high-pressure jobs, mothers of young children, and homeschooling moms especially need to do this because of the constant, dawn-to-dusk demands of their situations. A high-performing single woman I know, who pours herself into others, retreats to a coffee shop regularly. She chooses a window seat and loves to relax with a good book, an audio sermon, or just staring out the window and thinking. "There's something about a local café and my love for coffee," she said, "that creates a positive environment for my mind." She finds music especially soul refreshing: "Anything from classical, Christian contemporary, old hymns, and psalms— listening to music is therapeutic for my mind and helps me pace myself throughout the day."

It's particularly difficult to implement such times alone

---

9. "Seen at 11: She Sheds," CBS New York, https://www.youtube.com/watch?v= -_Dkmyj2ZOg.

when kids are around because they want and need mom's attention and care. You can't just say to the injured two-year-old, "I'm having my she hour. See ya later." But here are a few solutions that have worked for me and others. First, if you have really young children, you can use their naptime to have your she hour. Using that precious hour to perfect the house just drains you even further, and it's going to be turned upside down again anyway.

Second, ask a friend or an older woman with fewer demands upon her time to come look after your children for an hour a couple of times a week. Such an arrangement need not be permanent, but it can be helpful until you get replenished.

Third, dads can try to get home from work earlier and do the bathing and bedtime routine, allowing mom an hour of filling instead of another hour of draining the gas tank.

Fourth, use a play yard to safeguard your children, then a baby gate as they get a bit older. I have done this with all five of our children. For an hour every morning I put them in their bedrooms and closed the gate for an hour, while I remained close enough to hear them. For the first few days they screamed the house down, but then they got used to it and even began to look forward to it. It gave them a chance to play with their toys without older siblings interfering.

Some think caging or "imprisoning" kids behind a gate is torture. But not doing it can be torture of yourself. As Dr. Greer said, when you're depleted, you need to refuel in order to give to others again. Additionally, kids learn to be imaginative and creative when they are left to entertain themselves. They discover how to be content and happy in their own little world for an hour.

Most women who start a she hour to help them heal eventually make it a permanent part of their daily lives. They come to view it almost as a mini vacation each day, something they can look forward to, enjoy at the time, and draw benefit from throughout the rest of the day. A counselor told one of my friends to remember the preflight instructions for oxygen masks: "Put your own mask on first and then your children's." She shed time is putting on the oxygen mask so we can be a better mom for our kids, a better wife for our husband, a better employee for our employer, and therefore a better servant for Christ.

### Using Your She Hour

How should you use your she hour? Take your pick from hobbies, crafts, gardening, reading—anything that breaks the monotony and boredom of motherhood or that relieves the stress and pressure of working life. Ideally it's something that gives you so much pleasure that you forget yourself, your circumstances, and your responsibilities, leaving you renewed and refreshed. Some hobbies need more than an hour, of course. In Scotland, David would sometimes look after the children while I went out fishing on a quiet river every couple of weeks. Even if I came back with an empty net, it was so good to empty my mind and think about nothing for a few hours.

Crafts, like hobbies, help to meet the very human need to see some results from our work—which is often frustratingly rare in many workplaces and in our day-to-day parenting and home management. One young woman I know enjoys small DIY projects. "I often like to refurbish small furniture pieces or anything that involves working with wood. I also enjoy putting together little gift baskets for my college friends who are away from home or any friend who might need some encouragement. It's something little, but it's a way to serve others while I'm at it." Then there's my hyper-fit friend, whose idea of a she hour is to hit the gym, pump iron, and break sweat. We're all so different, aren't we?

If you're lacking imagination and creativity, check out a resource such as Pinterest. At our church, single and married ladies of all ages organize a monthly Pinterest night, which often develops into another opportunity for grace-filled and refreshing fellowship. To those, like me, who are not naturally crafty, these ladies bring their ideas and skills, while we all enjoy friendship. We have fellowship, and we have creativity, and we are bound together as sisters in the Lord.

My favorite she-hour activities are reading in the winter and yardwork in the warmer months. This may sound weird, but I especially love pulling weeds. Maybe it's the opportunity to see some progress and order in the dirt even when there's none in the kitchen. I also find reading real paper books especially relaxing. It stimulates my mind and yet calms it at the same time. Facebooking or iPadding around the Internet stimulates the mind but also drains it further, mainly because the mind is constantly dotting from one thing to another rather than resting on one subject or interest for a time. In *How Changing Your Reading Habits Can Transform Your Health*, Michael Grothaus explains, "Reading doesn't just improve your knowledge, it can help fight depression, make you more confident, empathetic, and a better decision-maker."[10] A young friend of mine who has found reading especially therapeutic explained the kind of books that help her relax:

---

10. Michael Grothaus, "How Changing Your Reading Habits Can Transform Your Health," Fast Company, July 27, 2015, http://www.fastcompany.com/3048913/how -to-be-a-success-at-everything/how-changing-your-reading-habits-can-transform-your -health.

"Something that is a light read, a little educational, but with a great and captivating storyline."

Maybe you've noticed that men don't seem to have any difficulty in setting aside time for a man hour, whether it's watching football, snoozing on the sofa, shooting hoops, or whatever. That's because men think about fewer things at a time and are also better at shutting things out of their minds. They can teach us a thing or two. A she hour isn't selfish. It's loving yourself as your neighbor. As Matthew Henry explains:

> There is a self-love which is corrupt, and the root of the greatest sins, and it must be put off and mortified; but there is a self-love which is the rule of the greatest duty: we must have a due concern for the welfare of our own souls and bodies. And we must love our neighbour as truly and sincerely as we love ourselves.[11]

As she shed owner Barbara Teckles observed: "If women can find a spot of their own to collect themselves again and to get some peace and quiet, everyone is going to benefit from that."[12]

### Weekly Refreshment

One of the most common deficits in the lives of people I've counseled with depression is the absence of a regular weekly sabbath. By "sabbath," I mean a joyful day of rest and re-freshment centered on the worship of God, the fellowship of his people in the local church, and the renewing of family relationships. I firmly believe that one of the greatest causes of stress, anxiety, burnout, and depression in our modern

11. Matthew Henry, *Exposition of the Bible*, Matthew 22:40.
12. "Seen At 11: She Sheds."

culture is a failure to receive the sabbath pattern (six days of work, one day of rest) as the gift of a wise and compassionate God. As Jesus himself said, "The Sabbath was made for man" (Mark 2:27)—and that includes women. Observing sabbath rest is especially important in the New Testament era, since the Sabbath moral principle has been shorn of the temporary trappings of Israel's ceremonial and civil law.

Yet, as a female student friend at a Christian university discovered, sabbath rest is not a familiar concept even in the Christian church. "Our professor asked the students to 'Raise your hand if you are currently practicing a sabbath rest.' Two out of twenty-eight students raised their hands, and I was one of them. This blew my mind! It seems as though my generation does not understand the biblical principle of sabbath rest." She went on to say, "The Sabbath has been a huge factor in preventing further burnout in my life. I can't stress enough how public worship, private worship, and physical rest on a weekly basis renew my spirit and motivate me to live with purpose for the kingdom."

Even secular sources are increasingly recognizing the need for a weekly sabbath. The *Atlantic* article, "*The Case for the Sabbath, Even if You're Not Religious*," makes the case for a sabbath even if God has nothing to do with it by promoting the social, psychological, and productivity benefits of a weekly day of rest.[13] *Sabbath Manifesto* was developed by "artists, writers, filmmakers, and media professionals who, while not particularly religious, felt a collective need to fight back against our increasingly fast-paced way of living." They

---

13. Menachem Kaiser, "The Case for the Sabbath, Even if You're Not Religious," *The Atlantic*, March 30, 2010, https://www.theatlantic.com/entertainment/archive/2010/03/the-case-for-the-sabbath-even-if-youre-not-religious/38187/.

urge "one day per week to unwind, unplug, relax, reflect, get outdoors, and get with loved ones."[14]

How much more beneficial is a weekly sabbath if we put its Maker at the center of it. It's a gift, not a threat. It's a time for healing the body, the mind, the soul, and our relationships with God and others. It's God's way of providing us with a spiritual and eternal perspective on our lives. It's God's gift of margin in our lives, and therefore we need feel no guilt in embracing that one day in seven in its entirety. Just like our muscles need a rest after working out, so our lives become more productive if we take God's provided rest.

I'm not going to prescribe details of how this sabbath principle should be worked out in your own life—our circumstances are all so different—but let me simply share with you what David and I do, to get you thinking about what would work best for you. We try to avoid a late bedtime on Saturday evening so that we are refreshed on Sunday morning. When we wake up on Sunday, we each have our own devotional reading and prayer time, followed by a fairly leisurely breakfast and family worship.

We go to church for the 9:30 a.m. service (I often long for the 11:00 a.m. start time in Scotland that allowed a longer time in bed), and we are there until about midday, by the time the various Sunday schools are over. We don't rush away from church but take plenty of time to enjoy chatting with our brothers and sisters in the Lord and to encourage our children in their church friendships.

Once we get home, we have coffee and cookies, and the seven of us sit around chatting about church, the sermon, what

---

14. http://sabbathmanifesto.org/.

we've been reading in the Bible, and just life in general. The family helps me get Sunday lunch together, and then David shares with the kids Christian videos he's collected through the week. These might be testimonies, news items that have a Christian angle, Christian songs—really, anything that David thinks could be spiritually profitable or help discussion.

We then have a slow lunch with all our kids, after which we have a couple of hours of quiet for napping, reading, a short walk, or lying in the sun. Maybe our son Allan will play his guitar and lead us in singing worship songs. We then go to church for the evening service. After more fellowship, we return home with our younger kids for bacon and eggs, and our older kids go to their youth group. Then we have an early bedtime to set us up for the coming week, and that's it.

Everything is done slowly, calmly, and quietly. For me, it's been a lifesaver. For ministry families, Sunday is usually one of the busier days, and therefore it may be best to choose a regular weekday in order to honor the sabbath principle of one day's rest.

## Annual Refreshment

The last refreshment stop is an annual vacation. Does that sound weird—vacation and refreshment in the same sentence? For many of us, it seems like a contradiction. We feel guilty leaving our work undone for a few days. It seems easier not to go on vacation because of all the preparation and all the catchup on our return. Those of us with families perhaps look back on previous vacations when the kids got sick or had accidents. But despite these difficulties, I wouldn't miss our annual vacation, because it's another key element of refreshment for me and, indeed, for my whole family.

Over the years, yes, we've ended up in the emergency room with injured kids. We've taken wrong turns and ended up lost. I've left my daughter's insulin in the fridge and had to do multiple phone calls to be able to secure some in a pharmacy hundreds of miles from home. We've been soaked, and we almost floated away in a tent. We've been stuck on a yacht in the Mediterranean with thunder and lightning flashing and crashing in a deafening melee; but we have so much to talk and laugh about and to thank God for, especially when we look back at the photos and videos.

Before being married, a teacher friend of mine used to go on vacation with a couple of her colleagues. It was a good time to de-stress from school business together. Some singles I know like to go to a family camp and be refreshed by interaction with a wide range of ages. Still others in my circle love mission trips or group vacations to historic Christian sites.

Over the years, I've discovered four keys to a refreshing vacation. First is to have minimal travel to and from our destination and during the vacation. That may mean vacationing near to home or using air travel to cut down on travel time. It also means staying put and not dashing around here, there, and everywhere. Remember, it's about refreshment, not more achievement. Relax, slow down, enjoy socializing, and take your foot off the accelerator.

Second, learn to sit still. In my early days of marriage, and before kids, I could hardly sit still on vacation for two minutes. I was so used to living on the end of a hospital pager that it was hard to relax and soak up the sun, even with a book. David, on the other hand, loved to sit for hours with a book or the newspaper. Our compromise was to rest in the morning with a book beside a pool, a lake, or on a beach, and then do something active in the afternoon, such as hiking. Twenty-five years later, my kids want to get going, get moving, and get some action, and I have joined David on the sun loungers with a book for hours, wondering where the kids get all their energy. But we still follow roughly the same pattern. We spend the mornings relaxing and use the afternoons to do some local sightseeing and other activities.

Third, have a kitchen rotation. If you're camping or staying in an apartment, plan your vacation so that your friends or husband and kids take on some of the cooking and cleaning duties. Maybe eat out every third or fourth day. The aim is to avoid simply being chief cook and bottlewasher in a different venue.

Fourth, take sufficient time. We've found a week is too little to really unwind and get benefit. But anything longer than two weeks, and David and I are itching to get back to work. So somewhere between ten and fourteen days seems to be the ideal. However, don't rule out mini getaways. A young woman in my church told me how much she benefitted from a road trip with her sister. "Just last year, my sister and I traveled to the outlet mall in Michigan City, Indiana, and also went to the beach for a few hours. I really loved this mini getaway, and I think she did too."

Vacations make memories, memories that you cannot make at home. Vacations bind friends and families together in a unique way. Vacations take you to churches you never knew existed and Christians you never met before. Vacations make you pray for these other Christians. Vacations show you more of God's world and the power of the gospel in other people's lives. Vacations enrich your spiritual life. Vacations make you laugh together. Vacations make you reminisce together. Vacations show you God's protection on strange roads in strange places. I heard of one Christian couple who decided to have a staycation one year, staying at home and doing absolutely nothing for a whole week. They found it to be an utterly miserable experience. So get away!

## Seasonal Refreshment

In addition to these daily, weekly, and annual refreshings, we should also recognize longer seasons of life that call us to adjust our pace. As Solomon said, "To everything there is a season, a time for every purpose under heaven" (Eccles. 3:1). He identified twenty-eight of them (vv. 2–8). Most of us will have fewer, but identifying our season of life—marriage, motherhood, menopause, retirement, bereavement, loss, relocation, and so on—and adjusting accordingly helps us to move wisely and confidently through each season at a grace-paced speed. When my friend Sarah read an early draft of this book she sent me this note:

> As women especially, we can't forget that our hormones (cycles, pregnancy, nursing, menopause) add something into the mix that shouldn't be ignored. Just because we can't control it doesn't mean we shouldn't account for it. I have had a tendency to look at what I can't control and just blaze past it like it doesn't matter since I can't really do anything about it anyway. But it does matter, and it does have an impact, and I will have to make adjustments at times, even if I don't like it.

She views "identifying your season" as a means of accepting reality and working with it, not against it, admitting, "I've made the mistake in the past of thinking, 'Well, this is just how it is so I have to deal with it' and thinking that that means I essentially have to ignore the constraints of my new season and operate at the same level I was before, afraid to make excuses."

## From Going and Going to Grace and Grace

A grace-paced life involves recognizing God's grace in all the different refreshment stops he has placed for us along life's way. As I reflect on my own story and a number of women's stories I've heard over the years, one phrase crops up again and again: "I just kept going and going and going." Imagine if you saw a marathon runner utterly exhausted and yet refusing every drink of water the organizers had provided along the way. You'd think she was crazy. God's grace is also seen in these refreshment stops that allow us time for reflection. We leave behind our frantic pace of life for a time to recalibrate our speed, to get a perspective on where we are going and why. We pause to remember God's role in our lives, to worship him for his all-sufficient grace, and to keep our eye on the ultimate horizon of eternity. One of the Devil's best weapons is noise. Just as people use white noise to block out other noise, Satan uses lifestyle noise to block out God's voice. "Be still and know that I am God."

As we enjoy the benefits of a quieter inner and outer life and build God-given refreshings of grace into our lives, we find time to pause, to calm down, and to think about who we are and why we are here, questions that will be answered in the next two stations.

Station 6

# Rethink

↻

Every two seconds, someone's identity is snatched through fraud, with 15.4 million Americans falling victim to identity theft in 2016 at a total annual loss calculated at $36 billion.[1] Little wonder that a sizeable industry has developed offering various identity-theft protection schemes, with some offering to restore your identity if it does end up being stolen.

Although the statistics indicate that one in four Americans has experienced identity theft, the reality is actually far worse.[2] All of us, to one degree or another, have had our identity stolen by thieves far more skillful and subtle than Chinese hackers and Russian phishers. These thieves include: pride, commercials, Hollywood, Pinterest, Facebook, supermodels, (super)mommy blogs, public schools, homeschool superfamilies, fashion, peer pressure, disappointment, failure, the Devil, aging, bereavement, illness, false theology, and on and on.

1. Brandon Gonzalez, "Identity Theft Targeted in Anti-Fraud Effort," WBFO Morning Ed., April 26, 2017, http://news.wbfo.org/post/identity-theft-targeted-anti-fraud-effort.

2. LifeLock, https://www.lifelock.com/.

These thieves are more dangerous because they steal the answer to the second-most important question in the world: "Who am I?" (The first being "Who is God?") Our answer to that question determines the way we view ourselves; the way we think, speak, and act; and the nature of our relationships with God and others. It also determines whether we live a life of stress and anxiety or a life that is grace-paced and grace-filled.

In this chapter we'll explore and examine false identities and their impact upon us and then recover and restore our true God-given identity. We'll start by looking at a short answer to the question "Who am I?" and then move on to a lengthier, more detailed answer.

## The Short Answer

Although very few of us are going around consciously thinking, "Who am I?" all of us are unconsciously answering that question every day of life. Although we're usually unaware of it, we are designing and building an identity, a way we think about ourselves and how we want others to think about us too. What we want to do here is identify that identity. Let's begin by writing out the phrase that springs to mind when we ask ourselves, "Who am I?" To help you get started, I've highlighted some examples that demonstrate how our basic sense of identity can have far-reaching effects.

### Isabel the Immoral

Isabel was converted to Christ in her late twenties after spending much of her teens and twenties in numerous immoral relationships—some long-term, many short-term, but all sinful. Now that she's a believer in Christ, she cannot shake off the immoral identity that defined her existence for so long. She feels dirty and ashamed when she is with other Christian women who kept themselves pure until marriage, and she doubts she will ever be married because she is "soiled goods." She hears sermons about "whiter-than-snow" forgiveness, but light gray is about the best she can hope for.

## Frances the Facebooker

Ever since Frances joined Facebook as a teenager, she has experimented with many personas and identities to uncover the most popular or attention getting. Her self-worth is tied up with the number of friends, followers, and "likes" she has on social media. Those who know her best do not recognize the person they see on Facebook or in the home and meals she posts on Pinterest.

## Vickie the Victim

Vickie was abused as a child. She didn't talk about it for many years, bottling up the pain and suffering in silence. When she did eventually open up and seek biblical counseling, healing began to take place through the power of God's Word and Spirit. However, that healing has stalled because another counselor advised Vickie to talk much more publicly and frequently about her abuse. However, with every telling, the wounds that God had been healing are picked raw. Instead of taking on the identity of Vickie the victor, triumphing over suffering by God's grace, she has become Vickie the victim, reliving her suffering again and again.

### Fiona the Failure

Fiona did everything right, but her children have gone all wrong. Although she parented by the book and devoted herself to being a godly mother, her three children all left the church in their late teens and are living worldly lives. Her hopes and dreams have been dashed, her whole purpose for living smashed. Whatever else she has done or will do in life, she sees herself as a failure with a capital F.

### Susan the Strong

Susan's dad was a driven, tough, and successful man with similar high standards for his children. Susan unconsciously, though understandably, adopted this identity—strong, a driver, a hard worker—and carried this with her into adult life. She's just turned forty-five, however, and she's struggling to maintain the same level of energy and productivity at work. Her mind doesn't seem to be as sharp or efficient as it once was, and she's getting palpitations and chest pain from time to time. But because she is Susan the Strong, she keeps pushing and driving herself, resulting in constant fatigue and frustration at her limitations.

### Paula the Perfectionist

Paula is a homeschooling mother of five whose ideal family looks like the idyllic pictures on the back of homeschooling books. Her aim is to sew her own clothes, bake her own bread, make her own soap, can her own fruit, exercise daily, and have all her children married by twenty-one. Except none of these things is happening. She's accomplishing a lot every day—in the homeschool, in the kitchen, in the church, and in her community—but because she can't do everything, she feels she's a failure at everything. A young single friend explained to me how debilitating this perfectionism can be: "There's nothing that bothers me more than missing devotions, getting a poorer grade than I know I was capable of, missing a basket in basketball practice, or even bringing a car up to a customer at work and it still has a small smudge on it despite my best efforts. I want God's approval, my family's approval, my church's approval, my professor's approval—and the list could go on."

### Cindy the Sinner

Cindy's church specializes in law, sin, and judgment, with justification, forgiveness, and adoption barely getting a mention. Her pastor is an expert on what's wrong with Christians, with the church, and with the world. Although she thinks she was saved a number of years ago, she has little or no assurance of faith but plenty of confidence that she's a sinner and deserving of God's wrath. Her children are puzzled about their mom, unable to figure out why being loved by God and going to heaven are so depressing.

### Justine the Just A . . .

I've met so many Justines. When I worked as a doctor, nearly all my female patients who worked exclusively at home would answer the vocational question with "I'm *just* a housewife," or "I'm *just* a homemaker," or "I'm just a secretary." At the root of this answer is an unbiblical view of vocation, the wrong idea that only ministry callings are divine callings, that only overtly Christian work is worthwhile work, or that only certain kinds of work outside the home count as a vocation. Justine has never read what William Tyndale wrote: "If our desire is to please God, pouring water, washing dishes, cobbling shoes, and preaching the Word is all one."[3] Martin Luther once said, "God and the angels smile when a man changes a diaper." If God takes pleasure in a man changing one diaper, how much more when you are changing ten a day?[4]

*Far-Reaching Consequences*

I've given you these examples not only to help you discover your own basic identity but also to show you how easy it is to have your identity stolen, distorted, or changed by various events, decisions, and circumstances. It also demonstrates how our answer to the question, "Who am I?" can have such far-reaching consequences for many years. Getting the right answer to that question, thinking about ourselves as God wants us to think about ourselves, is one of the most important activities in Refresh Gym and is a vital step toward living a grace-paced life.

## The Long Answer

Given our complexity, none of us can be fully defined by a short phrase. That's why we now need to dig a bit deeper and provide a more detailed answer to the question, "Who am I?" So, this time, instead of a short phrase, write out all the words that come to mind when you think about who you are. Try to answer the question from a long-term, objective perspective rather than on short-term feelings that can change

---

3. William Tyndale, cited in Os Guinness, *The Call* (Nashville: Thomas Nelson, 2003), 34.
4. Martin Luther, cited in Guinness, *The Call*, 34.

on any given day, depending on whether it's an up day or a down day. One aim of this exercise is to help you reach and embrace a stable sense of identity that will prevent multiple identity crises arising from daily feelings and events.

To get you started, here are the words that came into my mind when I answered the question. I didn't try to be theologically or politically correct, and I recorded the words in the order that they occurred: mother, pastor's wife, Christian, sporty, happy, energetic, sociable, helpful, taxicab, self-critical, organized, introspective, doctor, late, stressed, worried, failure.

Spend some time on your list; the first ten words or so will come relatively quickly, while the rest will take longer. And once you've got your list, stand beside me and learn as I recover and rebuild my true identity in eight steps that will transform the way we think about ourselves.

### Reorder Priorities

The first problem I notice is the order of my answers. Like many women, I have the tendency to define myself by my family (others might define themselves by their job). That's what came first to my mind—my children and my husband. That's a problem for a number of reasons, not least because God defines people first by their spiritual state and then by their spiritual character. It's also a problem because—what happens when my children grow up, or make terrible choices, or if my husband dies? These natural relationships must come second to our spiritual relationship with God. Our spiritual status and character must come before everything else. That's what came first to the apostle Paul's mind when he thought about himself: "By the grace of God I am what I am" (1 Cor. 15:10). When I discussed this with my friend Sally, she related:

> All through my childhood years and even into adulthood I struggled with the label of PK [pastor's kid]. I often felt like people were looking at me and how I was acting morally. "But you shouldn't be acting that way, Sally; your dad's a minister!" was what I, and my other six siblings, would hear often. Then I got married to my husband and, soon after, received the label "doctor's wife." I thought both of these labels came with certain expectations. But I have learned more and more every year that these are just a part of who I, Sally, am. Most importantly I am a daughter of the King! Then I have a lot of other roles too: wife, mother, friend, sister, neighbor, and church member.

There's more reordering to be done within these categories (for example, being a wife should come before being a mother), but I hope it's obvious how the *priorities* of our identity will impact our thoughts, words, and actions (or lack of them).

### Expand Incompletes

Next, we want to find where our self-descriptions are incomplete and expand them so they influence us much more. The most obvious candidate for expansion in my identity is "Christian." That's true, but so much more could be added. The Bible uses many different words and metaphors to describe the Christian: forgiven, redeemed, accepted, justified, adopted, heir, blessed, seated in heavenly places, sealed with the Spirit, in Christ, and so on (see Ephesians 1). If I expand "Christian" by adding these grace-driven descriptions to my list, this part of my identity will have much more influence on my self-image. A grace-filled identity will produce a grace-paced life.

## Fill in Gaps

The more I've thought about my long answer, the more I've realized that there are some significant gaps, parts of my identity that I did not include, perhaps because I did not want to admit them, as they involve some of my besetting sins. But for the sake of accuracy, I have to include these significant weaknesses. For example, I am defensive, I am anxious, and I am susceptible to depression. Unless I recognize these weaknesses as part of me, I won't take the necessary steps to address them.

On the other hand, I also left out some of my strengths. That's probably because, in my Scottish culture, talking about oneself in a positive way is discouraged. But if God has given us a strength or an ability, it is part of our God-given identity; we should recognize it, thank God for it—though probably not on Facebook—and see this aspect of our identity as part of the way God guides us into his calling for us. God has made me empathetic, patient, and hardworking, and I enjoy serving and helping people. No surprise then that God led me into the medical profession and made me a pastor's wife. Again the apostle Paul is our model of balance here. He acknowledged the weakness of his past record (1 Cor. 15:9), but he also asserted that he was the hardest-working apostle—by the grace of God, of course (1 Cor. 15:10).

## Prosecute Falsehoods

Although there were times when the apostle Paul did not respond to the slanderous attacks on his character and identity that were circulated by his enemies, there were other times when he went to war against them. Throughout 2 Corinthians he prosecuted the falsehoods that were threatening to undermine his ministry. He exposed the lies, named them, presented evidence against them, found them guilty, sentenced them to exile, and drove them out of the church. In doing so, he provided a pattern for us to follow in dealing with false accusations, especially those that come from within. Here are two examples of how I prosecute falsehoods concerning my self-identity and replace them with truth.

*I am servant of all.* Notice that in my long answer, I put *helpful* as part of my identity. The truth is that although I love serving people, *helpful* often morphs into "I am a servant to all." I feel I have to say yes to everyone and everything (notice the next word in the list is *taxicab*). I put myself second most of the time and spend my life running around trying to do everything and please everybody—which, of course, is not just impossible but extremely damaging. God has called me to serve a limited number of people—primarily my family—in a limited number of ways, and I have to accept that I cannot do everything that I think everybody wants me to do. I also have to be able to recognize my limitations and my need of others to serve my needs as well. "I am servant of all" needs to be prosecuted, found guilty, executed, and replaced with "I am a servant with limitations."

*I am in total control.* I put *organized* on my list because I do love to be organized and have everything in its place. But sometimes my gift of organization can slide into "I am in total control," an ability possessed only by God. Not only do I want every piece of paper, every bottle, every plate, every book, every shirt, and every toy in the right place, but I want my timetable and my family to be similarly neat and tidy. Yes, I just built my own internal stress machine that can run 24/7. Without giving up personal responsibility and family discipline I need to realize that total control is a myth, a falsehood, that will never be realized for more than one second of my life. Releasing personal control and handing total and ultimate control over to God dismantle the stress machine and let me live a calmer, more grace-paced life, doing what I can but trusting God to do what I cannot.

An example is my struggle to release my children into God's care. Although my twenty-one-year-old son has good friends who love just hanging out together at each other's homes, I used to lie awake until he was home, thinking that to go to sleep would be irresponsible. Meanwhile, David snored away happily. A year ago, my son joined the Marine Corps and ended up on the other side of the country with guys I knew nothing about. I have no control whatsoever, and yet I sleep soundly every night after committing him to the Lord in prayer. I've released him into God's care—but I could have chosen to do it when he was living with us in Grand Rapids rather than being forced into it when he moved away. This has been a good lesson in handing control to the Controller.

## Add Balance

Part of my identity is "I am a sinner." I can't deny this and never want to. But it's not the whole truth. The apostle Paul also instructs me to think of myself as "dead to sin" (Rom. 6:11). Why is this balancing statement so important? The apostle understood that if I only think of myself as a sinner, then I will sin. However, if I also view myself as dead to sin, the more dead to sin I will be. If when temptation comes knocking, all I say is, "I'm a sinner," I'm most likely going to succumb. But if I say, "No, I'm dead to sin and alive to Christ," I am more likely to die to the sin and live to Christ.

A Christian woman I know once lost her temper with her husband while I was sitting with them. Eventually a little embarrassment set in, and she turned to me and said, "I'm a bit short-fused, but so was my mother." What hope did she have of beating this sin if she just kept excusing it (as she frequently did)? Instead of telling herself she was a sinner—and therefore, of course, succumbing to anger—she should have been reckoning herself dead to sin, dead to anger, when the temptation arose. Imagine how many more victories we would have over sin if we identified not just as a sinner but as dead to sin.

### Accept Change

You'll notice that I put *doctor* well down on my list. When I worked full-time, *doctor* would have been much more prominent in my sense of identity. It slipped down the list a bit when kids came along and I reduced my practice to one morning a week and a few evenings in the month. I haven't practiced medicine since I came to the States years ago, so it is now near the end of the list. It's still part of my identity, as it was such a large part of my life (and because I am still frequently asked for medical advice), but I have adapted and accepted the change.

We can cause ourselves huge problems if we do not accept change in our age, abilities, status, relationships. In my teens, I would have put *athlete* at number two or three in my long answer, as I loved running, competing in races, and playing soccer. If I still put that as a primary part of my identity, I'd be either lying or dying.

Some women I know struggle to accept change in their identity when they stop working in a professional career and give themselves to full-time parenting. They were used to everything being organized at clearly demarcated time intervals, their work space being tidy, their clothes always smart, and clocking off at the same time to go home to relax. Suddenly, they find themselves in a situation where demands are incessant and the interruptions unpredictable, and clocking off rarely happens. It's hard even to dress professionally as they used to. But when God gives grace to accept and adapt to that change in identity, mothers can stop looking back with regret, stop looking at other women with envy, and give up trying to look like a CEO with three kids hanging off their pantsuit.

## Reframe Failure

I've known failure in my life and would probably have put *failure* as number one on the list when I finally conceded that I was not able to homeschool my oldest child past ninth grade, which is when we decided to send him to school. I put *failure* last on my list now though, because although I've known some failures since then, I no longer let failure define me. Indeed, I see it in a different light because God has taught me so much good through failure: humility, dependence, patience, and compassion for others' failures. All things work together for our good, including failures (Rom. 8:28).

It's as if God's overruling providence puts a golden frame around our failures, turning them into something useful and productive. Above all, my failures bring me to the feet of the perfect Lord Jesus in worship. When I count up all my failures even in a week and then think that he lived for thirty-three years in the midst of such challenges and provocations and never failed once, I cannot but worship and adore him. He succeeded where I failed and imputed his success to me so that I no longer see my whole identity through the lens of my failures. I've failed, but it doesn't define me. I still fail, but he still loves me and accepts me. One of my daughter's friends who has battled perfectionism for several years on a number of fronts traced her victory against this foe to a time when "God continued to reveal more of my sin and more of himself, which gave me a clearer and more biblical perspective of my true identity."

*Anticipate the Future*

It's painful to watch celebrities and athletes whose best days are behind them and yet who are vainly trying to hold on to them. The beautiful actress spends more time at the plastic surgeon's than in front of the camera. The gold-medal gymnast spends more time on the treatment table than on the beam. They once had identities that brought them fame and fortune, but as these identities fade, so do their popularity and their bank balances. Their best days are behind them, sometimes long behind them, but they won't accept it and, as various reality shows prove, will do anything to relive them. For Christians, though, our best days are ahead of us. Yes, we try to recover and rebuild our identity in this world, but we look forward to a day when we will enjoy a far better identity in the world to come.

The apostle John crystallized this for us in these words: "Behold what manner of love the Father has bestowed on us, that we should be called children of God! . . . Beloved, now we are children of God" (1 John 3:1–2). What a glorious present identity—"God's children"! But there's something even better in the future: "It has not yet been revealed what we shall be, but we know that when He is revealed, we shall be like Him, for we shall see Him as He is" (v. 2). We will one day be like Christ! Imagine that being part of your identity—being like Christ. It doesn't get better than that. What a prospect to think about.

So, yes, let's try to recover our stolen identity by rebuilding it on scriptural foundations: reordering priorities, expanding incompletes, filling in gaps, prosecuting falsehoods, adding balance, accepting change, and reframing failure. By doing so, we change not only our thoughts for the better but our feelings, our words, and our actions too. But let's also anticipate the indescribable prospect of being like Jesus. If we add to our identity, "I'm going to be like Jesus," that will have a tremendous present impact upon us because "everyone who has this hope in Him purifies himself, just as He is pure" (v. 3).

One of the great benefits of a clear sense of identity is that we can then more easily identify and clarify our life purposes and make plans to accomplish them, the exercise that awaits us at the next station.

# Reduce

**C**

Ms. Maxed-Out is in the gym, but she's carrying so many weights around that some of them are falling on her feet and on the floor. Your immediate thought is, *How is she going to use all these at the same time? Doesn't she know that there are racks for all these dumbbells and that you're allowed to focus on one exercise at a time?* When you look closely, you see her furrowed brow and hear her sighing. Your heart goes out to her, and you just want to put your arm around her and say, "Hey, this is no fun! Can I help you out, and together we can figure out a better system? Let's get rid of some of these weights. That way, you can enjoy your workout instead of its being a miserable chore."

Upstairs at the Kid Zone, a little girl runs along the corridor and flies into the room, excited to play with some little friends. No structure, no plan—just laugh, play, and imagine, then more laugh, play, and imagine. She loves it and always leaves grinning from ear to ear. At home, she runs out to the yard and basks in the freedom of more play. Do you remember when life was like that? No worries, no furrowed brow; just eat, sleep, and play. Not a care in the world!

I remember these days too, and at times I've wished I could go back to them, even for a short time. I've been Ms. Maxed-Out too often and little Miss Kid Zone too rarely. At times of extreme stress and anxiety, I've watched the birds and envied their carefree existence, fluttering worry-free from tree to tree. But as Jesus reminded us, God cares for his children more intimately than he does even the little sparrows (Matt. 6:25–34) and wants to free us from carrying unnecessary weights (1 Pet. 5:7). I want to help you embrace the freedom that our heavenly Father gives to live a grace-paced and grace-weighted life by reducing the weights that are dragging you down.

## Life Weights

Life creeps up on us, doesn't it? During our school years there are some temporary stresses—exams and boyfriends—but these are like feathers compared to the crushing and complex burdens that accumulate over the next twenty years. By the time we're forty, we're carrying mortgage and credit card debt, work problems, husband and children worries, health issues, church conflicts, car repairs, and health-care premiums, and on and on it goes.

All that didn't just happen the day after graduation. The weights accumulated imperceptibly; they multiplied a little every year until life slowly yet inexorably crushed us. Now, our minds are frazzled, our hearts are pounding, our bodies are breaking down, our relationships are straining, our sleep is declining, our quality of work is suffering, and our happiness is a distant memory. What happened to little Miss Kid Zone? Any way of getting back to that? Even sometimes?

Let's begin to answer these questions by looking at two very different ways to live. This will give us a base to clarify our purpose in life, plan our days, and prune nonessentials, and so reduce some of the life-creep that has overtaken and overwhelmed us.

## Two Ways to Live

According to *New York Times* columnist David Brooks, there are two ways of thinking about life: "the Well-Planned Life" and "the Summoned Life."[1] In his column he turned to an essay derived from a commencement address by Harvard Business School professor Clayton Christensen for a model of the Well-Planned Life. The Well-Planned Life is one in which we take time to find a clear purpose, then make appropriate decisions about how to spend our time and use our talents in light of that. The person living the Summoned Life, on the other hand, rejects the possibility of long-term life planning, but, as situations and circumstances arise, asks, "What are these circumstances summoning me to do? How should I react?" I'm sure most of us can recognize ourselves in one of these—or maybe both, depending on the day.

So, which is the best way to live? Based on the truth of being made in the image of God and therefore called to reflect, to some degree, his purposeful sovereignty, I believe that every Christian should build on the firm base of a Well-Planned Life. No Christian should be just a victim of events, a helpless cork tossed to and fro on the ever-changing ocean of circumstances and other people's expectations. God put each of us here for a specific reason, and we shouldn't just drift from day to day,

---

1. David Brooks, "The Summoned Self," *New York Times*, August 2, 2010, http:// www.nytimes.com/2010/08/03/opinion/03brooks.html.

from week to week, from year to year, frittering away our lives without any sense of direction and jumping every time someone holds a hoop in front of us. We must take our time and our talents to God and ask him, "What will you have me to do?" That simple prayer would save many of us from years of pointless ping-ponging from activity to activity, from demand to demand, and from expectation to expectation.

There is a danger, though, in the Well-Planned Life. It can make us insensitive and unresponsive to the needs of others. Everybody must accept an element of the Summoned Life. But what should the ratio be? Christ is a good model for us here. Although he knew exactly why he was on earth and what he was to do, he also allowed for spontaneity in responding to unexpected events. At times he refused to be diverted by people's demands, but at other times he stopped and met an urgent need. He lived the Well-Planned Life but also left space for the Summoned Life. He managed to strike the perfect balance at all times.

So how do we find the sweet spot? Although each of us will find a different mix depending on our characters and callings, there are three words that I believe can help all of us find the right balance, three words that will enable us to reduce the weights that often crush the life out of us: *purpose*, *plan*, and *prune*.

## Purpose

If we aim at nothing, we always hit it. But if we want to accomplish anything worthwhile, we need specific targets. I want to outline five particular areas of life where a clear sense of purpose will yield substantial dividends. These are our spiritual life, our family life, our vocational life, our church life, and our social life.

## Spiritual Life

What is your spiritual purpose? Do you know what you want to achieve in your spiritual life? Are there graces you want to cultivate or sins you want to conquer? Do you want to grow in knowledge of Christian doctrine, or do you want to improve in sanctification? Is there a Christian grace or gift that you want to develop? Maybe, like many Christians, you've never thought about these questions. You've just drifted along hoping for the best, but you've never actually clarified in your own mind where you are going or what it would look like to arrive. Perhaps you've made some progress in a number of areas, but you haven't noticed it and, therefore, are not encouraged by God's work in your life.

That's why I recommend praying and thinking about specific areas in which you want to grow. You could pick a doctrine to learn, such as justification, and find some good books and sermons to teach and challenge you. Or focus on a grace such as joy and find ways to cultivate and exhibit it. Maybe tell a friend or a family member what you are doing and ask them to challenge and encourage you when necessary. You could also target a sin such as covetousness and find different resources to fire at it. You might want to practice the gift of hospitality and aim to host a small group of people every month and cultivate Christian fellowship over a meal. There are so many possibilities, but without picking one or two spiritual aims, we will either go round in circles or make a millimeter of progress in a thousand different directions.

*Family Life*

For those of us who are mothers, our greatest family aim is the salvation of our children. We are to raise them for the Lord (Eph. 6:4). We don't just want a few short years on this earth with them; we want to spend eternity in heaven with them. If we have that purpose at the forefront of our minds, it will help us to reduce the weight of secular and cultural expectations, which often take over our lives and theirs. They're expected to excel at school, be accomplished musicians, win MVP at every sport, and get a scholarship for college. They must get a high-paying job and definitely marry someone who has a college degree and a good job. The result? We (and they) all end up with stress-filled days (and empty bank accounts), striving and sweating to ensure they achieve these things. But what's the point if, along the way, we lose sight of our children's souls and why they or we are even on this earth?

Our kids need our love, they need family stability, they need the evening supper table, they need Sunday for mental, spiritual, and bodily rest, and so do we. The more we expect of our kids, the more we expect of ourselves, and vice versa. We need balance; they need balance. Yes, they should develop their God-given talents, but does God require that we run from one kid's practice to another kid's practice, to games and meets, and skip family meals and family devotions most evenings of the week? If we do that, we've picked up the impossible weight of cultural and secular expectation and dropped the most important weight of all—the spiritual, emotional, and relational nurturing of our kids, which can only be done when we have time to be together and talk with one another without time pressure.

One of the greatest weights upon young mothers is the crushing load of modern child-rearing dogma. Never has there been more information available about how to raise kids, and yet never has there been more confusion. It starts before our kids are even born. We are overwhelmed with the number of pregnancy theories, baby delivery theories, food theories, immunization theories, baby sleep theories, baby stimulation theories, and so on. Balance is jettisoned for extremes, and for so many mothers, what should have been the most joyful time in their lives becomes the most miserable, guilt-ridden experience. Often missing in the equation is the simple question, "How can I, to the best of my ability, use God's modern provisions to give my baby and me the best hope of surviving and thriving?" That question helps us clarify our purpose and unload the weight of other people's ideology.

Moms, we need to relax. Reduce our expectations of ourselves and our children. Don't be a slave to ideology. Please talk to older moms, preferably those who have been on this road several times. Prayerfully use your common sense and embrace some of theirs. You and your family will get a clearer sense of spiritual purpose, you'll all learn how to live a grace-paced life, and you'll all have the hope of a grace-filled eternity together.

*Vocational Life*

I'm a mom of five children: three boys, age twenty-one, eighteen, and four; and two girls, age fourteen and thirteen. I also happen to be a pastor's wife and a homeschooler. I have a medical degree and worked in that field for a number of years. Which of these realms does God mean for me to be operating in at the moment? Clearly not all of them. Let me share how

I've thought through my choices in order to help you do the same, whatever your present calling—homemaker, business employee, or student.

*Homemaker.* I believe, on the basis of Scripture (Titus 2:5), that my present circumstances require me to prioritize homemaking at this stage in my life. That means I'm an organizer, delegator, operations manager, administrator-in-chief, supplies manager, head chef, cleaning supervisor, cab driver, counselor, shoulder to cry on, and chief hugger. If you are a homemaker, I am sure you can add a few more to your homemaking list, but that's a start.

But where do I start and what am I aiming at? It was easy in the past. Before the kids arrived, I aimed at perfect floors and closets, orderly cushions, empty laundry baskets, tidy bathrooms, and relaxed meals. Five kids later, my daily life is lost shoes, missing towels, laundry mountains, sticky floors, and the van that looks more like a sandy beach, candy store, and the gym "lost and found" all rolled into one. I can easily become discouraged by my inability to reach past perfection. A friend of mine narrated her experience of guilt and unrealistic expectations:

> It's like setting one goal and then scoring yourself on another. I said yes to making a nice dinner for the family, so that means I said no to playing dress-up with my daughter. Sometimes at the end of the day, I think I should have been able to do both. Or I said yes to taking another client, so that means I said no to doing the dishes during naptime. Sometimes that means that even though I've accomplished a lot, I'll still get mad that I didn't accomplish mopping the floors or whatever as well.

Here's the question about vocational purpose that's helped me to reduce this overwhelming weight: "Is my aim a perfect house characterized by cold sterility or a happy home filled with love and the presence of God?" We need a measure of order and discipline in our homes, but unless we accept a more realistic standard when our kids come, we will quickly become fretting Marthas rather than peaceful Marys.

*Educator.* Again, on the basis of Scripture (Deut. 11:18–20), I believe parents are responsible for the education of their children with the aim of preparing them for a happy eternity and for usefulness on this earth—in that order. Both purposes are important, but the first must have precedence. Having these clear aims helps me to decide where and how to educate them in the light of changing family cirumstances, limited finances, the needs of each individual child, and the impact of educational choices on others in the family. All of these factors have to be weighed when considering how to achieve our aims.

David and I decided that homeschooling was the best way to achieve these aims within our budget. However, we've also had to rethink that, such as when my own mental health was suffering or when we concluded that a child needed more than we could give. If homeschooling turns your home into an unhappy place, hindering your spiritual and emotional well-being, and that of your family, then you need to ask God for courage, wisdom, and resources to find a better way of fulfilling your educational aims.

*Wife of a pastor.* I'm not a pastor's wife, I'm the wife of a pastor. That means this role comes after my responsibilities as a homemaker and educator of my children. I'm thankful that the churches David has pastored have not placed too much expectation upon me as a pastor's wife. However, at times I've taken on responsibilities in that role that I've regretted accepting because of the negative impact on me and my family. By remembering my vocational priorities—homemaker first, home educator second, and wife of a pastor third—I am much freer to say no to church demands when I can see that it will damage our family life or my kids' schooling. But I do look forward to the season in life when I can be much more involved again. Saying no is possible even for those involved in megachurches, which are bound to have an abundance of needs, as one worship leader's wife told me:

> I don't feel pressure from leadership to be everywhere and do everything. I feel that it is recognized that at my current life stage, much of my "serving" role involves making it easy for my husband to do his job on the weekends, and my uniqueness and giftings are recognized—there is not one cookie-cutter way laid out for a ministry wife to support the church. This is an amazing blessing. At our last church, I did feel pressured to be there every time the doors were open, and that caused strain and eventually a complete lack of caring on my part because I couldn't keep up, so I eventually just gave up trying at all. That rebel behavior is unusual for me. That was near the beginning of the end of our time there and in hindsight was one of the first big signs that it was time to leave.

*Doctor.* Obviously, some wives and mothers have to work outside the home for various reasons. It may be to make ends meet, it may be for personal development, or it may be to keep up professional certification for a possible future need. When we immigrated to the US, we decided it was not worth the time or the money for me to get licensed to practice as a doctor here. However, when I practiced in the UK, there was so much work available that I could have practiced medicine full-time. So how did I decide what to take on and what to say no to?

First, I kept my spiritual and vocational purposes in view and in order. My spiritual welfare came first. Then my vocational priorities came into the equation. I was first a home-maker, then an educator, then the wife of a pastor. Doctor came fourth in my vocational priorities. Second, I asked myself these two questions: (1) Is material gain beyond what we need the main motive for my working? (2) Does it hinder our family because I am always worn out? David and I would regularly discuss these questions prayerfully and ensure that he could fill in at times for me without hindering his work. If working outside the home damages our spiritual life or undermines our family responsibilities, we need to reconsider our decisions.

Maybe your situation is not as complex as mine. Perhaps you are a single working woman and you have one vocation—your job or your business. Well, as you know, it's still a busy pressurized life, isn't it? One of my single friends told me that she gets asked to do far more than married women because, "Well, you have no family!" She found this was also true in the church, with her name frequently proposed for multiple committees and ministries. So how do you decide what to do? Again it comes back to questions about our purposes in life.

First, keep asking yourself, "What is my spiritual purpose, and is my workload and work rate hindering or helping that?" Second, "What is my vocational purpose?" If your vocational purpose is to serve God in the workplace, that's your primary place of Christian service, and you should do it with all your might (Eccles. 9:10). You should not feel guilty about saying no to other ministry or service opportunities if taking them on will prevent you from fulfilling your work responsibilities. Third, "Why am I doing this?" Discerning and purifying our motives will go a long way to helping us decide what career path to follow, what positions to accept, what hours to work, and how we work. If our primary purpose is money or climbing the corporate ladder, then we will make certain choices. If our primary purpose is to glorify God and serve others, we will make far better choices. It will also distinguish us from others and make them ask, "What makes you tick?" The same questions can be adjusted to fit student life too. The key to surviving and thriving is to identify what God wants you to do, in what order of priorities, and follow through.

*Church Life*

There's no shortage of opportunities to serve in your church, attend various Bible studies, and go to midweek meetings. The question is, apart from attending church on Sunday, what else should we be doing in our church, what events should we go to, and what hospitality should we offer?

Our answer depends on a number of factors. First, consider your season of life. If you are a mother in a busy household, a business owner, a full-time student, or a high-pressured employee, it's unlikely that you'll have much more than an hour or two a week for church life apart from Sunday services. Second, ask yourself why you are participating. When I've asked myself that question, I've often realized that I was going to activities, ministries, and events not for the Lord but to please other people and meet what I perceived to be their expectations of me. Just because one person is doing lots of evangelism or service projects doesn't mean that you should. Remember, you are already serving God in your own spiritual life, in your family life, and in your vocational life. That's a lot already.

I asked one of my single friends how she decides what service opportunities to accept and which to decline. She said, "I begin with prayer, then gauge the level of necessity, how vital this ministry is. After that I ask, 'What's the spiritual value for myself and others?' And then I weigh how much pleasure I would find in doing it."

### Social Life

The opportunities to socialize are endless, and others' expectations for your socializing are endless. Whether it's church circles, work circles, school circles, or community circles, if you have a must-do mentality or a default-yes mind-set every time you are asked to do something or invited to go somewhere, you may feel totally swamped.

By identifying life purposes in our social choices, we can better decide our capacity for socializing and friendships. Intentionality and clarity in our purposes and humble honesty about our limitations will not only make our decisions easier but will also help to quiet our accusing conscience that always demands more. We may decide to cultivate a limited number of friendships. Or we may decide on no more than two to three social occasions a week. We cannot be friends with everyone, and we cannot meet everyone's expectations. Bear in mind that our social purposes will change, as will all our other purposes, as we transition through different seasons in life.

## Plan

Having identified our life purposes in five major areas and decided on the weights we have decided to carry or leave behind, we now need a plan. We have to figure out what steps to take to accomplish our life purposes. I may want to do twenty lunges with twenty pounds of weight, but unless I have a graduated plan, I will never get there. So we look at our life purposes and ask, "What are the steps I need to take to get there?" Following are the stress-relieving steps I try to follow to turn my purposes into plans.

### Calendar

If it's not on the calendar, it's not going to happen. If activities related to my life purposes are not on the calendar, I'm clearly not serious about these life aims. Entering everything on a calendar also helps us to stop overpromising to ourselves or others, as we can see visually the impossibility of what we are trying to do. Overpromising is the fatal result of an overly optimistic view of our abilities plus an unrealistic estimate of our available time plus a desire to please other people. The result is megastress for the promise maker and usually huge disappointment for the promise recipients.

Being married with kids, I can't just plan my calendar in isolation. David and I spend some time each week, ideally before the week begins, coordinating our calendars, focusing mainly on the coming week but also looking at that week in the context of what has gone before and what will come after. This prevents clashes, shares family responsibilities, and increases mutual accountability. We are especially careful to make sure that we aren't away from home too many evenings during the week, that David is not accepting too many speaking invitations over weekends, and that I am not saying yes just to please other people. We both firmly believe that shepherding our children and nurturing our own relationship is our first priority, because it's in these family relationships that God primarily works.

Try to envisage what your preplanned schedule will look like when you actually begin to live it. It's so quick and easy to put multiple activities into our calendar, but it takes a lot longer to live them out. Take some time to conjure up in your mind what the day or week will look like before adding another commitment.

## Routine

One of the most common problems associated with stress and depression is a lack of routine. As God is a God of order, not of confusion (1 Cor. 14:33), we who are his image bearers will thrive best when our lives have a regular rhythm and routine for eating, sleeping, working, and playing. It's easier to have a routine if we work outside the home, because we have colleagues and a boss. If we are full-time homemakers, we have to work harder to impose routine on ourselves and our family. I've often noticed that when I am out of the routine, the kids misbehave. If I don't know what's happening next, they sense it, and things become chaotic. That's why so many mothers struggle during summer break. My kids usually ask me in the morning, "What's the plan today, Mom?" If I have it already written, then it's a whole lot easier to push back and avoid having my day's agenda vocalized for me.

*Prioritize*

"If you don't prioritize your life, someone else will."[2] If we want to do our own prioritizing, we begin by listing all our duties, activities, and aims and then, using our life purposes, put them in four categories:

1. *Definite do.* Your most important God-given responsibilities and commitments.

2. *Desire to do.* Activities you would like to do, hope to do, and some of which you will do after the definite do's are done.

3. *Delay do.* Worthy activities that you would love to do some day but have to postpone now, until you have space and time in your schedule.

4. *Don't do.* Things you either commit to stop doing or say no to in the future.

Our life purposes and life priorities should then be reflected on our calendar, an exercise that usually reveals whether we are being realistic or idealistic. As my mornings are my most productive times, that's when I do my most demanding physical and mental tasks. I usually go out in the afternoon to run errands and then return home in good time to cook the evening meal. In the evenings, David and the kids are usually home, and we enjoy time together as a family. Evenings are also often the best time for me to do my own thing, such as reading. I'm not saying that it always goes smoothly, but without a plan it never will.

---

2. Greg McKeown, *Essentialism: The Disciplined Pursuit of Less* (New York: Crown, 2014), 10.

But what if you're a young, single woman? Here's the reply of a Christian whom I've come to respect and love:

How do I prioritize? I often ask my parents. They have lived a lot longer than I have and have shown and proven their wisdom time and again. When I accepted a teaching job to do while in school next year, they provided a lot of encouragement and advice to help me balance next year's schedule. I have also created for myself a list of five questions when I'm deciding what to prioritize in my schedule:

- Does it allow for family to come first? Will I be able to have family dinner or devotions at all this week?
- Does this week's schedule allow for at least one meeting with a friend or mentee (for the purposes of fellowship and spiritual accountability)?
- Does this week's schedule allow an appropriate block of time for homework and other necessary tasks so that I don't become overwhelmed?
- Does this week have planned breaks every day? (A walk, a nap, time to read, etc.)
- Does this week's schedule clearly prioritize my relationship with God? Are the things I commit to able to be done for his glory and honor? Or will I be too distracted with my to-do list? Is there sufficient time for private meditation and prayer?

## Detail

I try to write out particular tasks for the day, including the kids' chores, schoolwork, administration, grocery trips, dentist visits, kids' sports, and regular workout sessions. If I can get my list sorted out the night before and entered on my calendar, the next day is likely to go more smoothly. The times I don't, I find myself going through the next day with an uncomfortable lack of clarity and even anxiety. Although it takes time to plan the details, I've found it saves time in the long run and prevents me living a Summoned-Life sort of day, the kind lived at the beck and call of my kids and others.

## Nothing

It's vitally important for all of us to title part of the day as "No Fixed Agenda." During summer breaks, I tell my kids that we will do one big thing each week, like go to the beach or hang out with our church friends. In a given week we will not go to the beach, play soccer, attend a birthday party, participate in VBS, and also go on a youth-group day trip. We structure weeks so as to have many lazy days, when we and our kids hang out at home. We play together and laugh and try to live a grace-paced life. We all need unstructured time. Sometimes the biggest accomplishment is to accomplish nothing.

## Audit

When we start the Reduce process, we need to take time at the end of each day to evaluate. Did we plan too much? Did we allow enough margin? Were we running around like headless chickens? Initially the comparison between the plan and the reality is a bit shocking, but slowly we'll align our expectations with reality, reducing frustration, disappointment, and stress.

Every few months or so, we need to make a big-picture assessment to see if we need to adjust to new circumstances. For example, we used to have family devotions directly after supper in the evening. Now, with our older children sometimes working late or attending college classes in the evening, we will often do devotions later, when everyone is home.

## Prune

We now come to the most painful part of the Reduce exercise. Having identified our life purposes and planned how to accomplish them, we must *remove* some things altogether in order to do the most important things well.

And the most important tool here is a two-letter word: *no*. Although it's one of the first words we learn as infants, it somehow becomes one of the hardest words for adults to say. Our plate is already full when we are asked to squeeze something else onto it. It's not a huge task on its own, but it's the tenth extra task we've added this week. We know we should say no, yet somehow yes leaves our lips. The result is that we do everything poorly and nothing well. The trivial many crowd out the vital few. It happens at home, at work, in the church, and in the clubs and societies we support. We are known as "yes-machines" and therefore get asked by everyone for everything.

Let me be blunt here. No matter how much of this book you implement, you will never refresh your life until you relearn how to say no and start saying it; and not just to the big things but to the small things too. "But," you might argue, "people won't like me if I say no to everything." It's not saying no to everything; it's saying no to some things. And saying yes to everybody may mean that you are saying no to God. As Jesus demonstrated, saying no to some people's plans for us allows us to say yes to God's will for us (Luke 12:13–14; John 2:4).

What's helped me prune with the sharp knife of *no* is to realize that I can live either trying to meet the unlimited needs and expectations of others or according to my limited capacity and my heavenly Father's expectations. If I try the former, I will work one hundred hours a week, still never meet every need or expectation, and end up overwhelmed, burned out, or worse. If I try the latter, I can work to my personal capacity with a good and peaceful conscience, even if people criticize or misunderstand me. With my life purposes in one hand and my limited capacity in the other, I can prune needs and expectations so that I am doing the most important things well and with joy, and I can have a sense of accomplishment as I enjoy some downtime.

## Magic Formula

Due to differences in our circumstances, there is no magic formula that fits all. What I can do is share with you the balance between the Well-Planned Life and the Summoned Life that works best for my character and responsibilities at this time in my life, an equation that is helping me accomplish what I believe is God's call for me, while at the same time remaining open to interruptions and unexpected events: 60 percent Well-Planned Life + 40 percent Summoned Life + 100 percent Prayerful Life. This doesn't make mathematical sense, but it does make spiritual sense. Without daily prayer for God's daily help, I can accomplish nothing.

We've now got a renewed sense of purpose, we have a plan about how to get there, and we've eliminated some of the unnecessary baggage we were carrying. Let's now pause at the next station and get refueled for the next stage of life's journey.

Station 8

# Refuel

↻

My husband once asked a Christian psychologist how he treats people with depression or anxiety. "Oh, that's easy," he replied; "I give them three pills." Inwardly, David groaned as multiple caricatures of pill-pushing doctors seemed to be sadly confirmed. After pausing for effect, however, the psychologist added, "Good exercise, good sleep, and good diet." The subsequent conversation made clear that he wasn't suggesting those three "pills" were the complete answer to every episode of depression or anxiety, but he was making the point that they are the fundamental building blocks of any long-term healing from mental and emotional ill-health. As we've already covered two of these "pills," good sleep and good exercise, we'll start by considering how the third one, good diet, helps to refuel rundown minds and moods. Then we're going to look at real pills, medications, and their potential role in refueling mental and emotional health. Last, we'll pour in some supplements by identifying activities that energize us.

## Food

I know most of you are tired of hearing about the latest food fads, extreme diets, and idealistic menu plans. Don't worry, so am I. Refresh Gym is all about finding a healthy balance between idealism and couldn't-care-less-ism. That rare and sparsely populated space of practical realism is what we're aiming at.

When I took up serious exercise again, I was surprised at my trainer's emphasis on eating the right food before and after exercise. That just wasn't a factor anyone thought about when I was running races a few decades ago. However, I've come to realize that just as my van won't move without gas and will be destroyed if I put diesel in it, so we all need regular refueling with the right kind of food if we are to run well. We've come a long way since entering Refresh Gym, and we've done a lot of repair work at each station. But much of that will be in vain if we don't fill up our tanks with premium gas. Our bodies and minds suffer from wear and tear and need to be reenergized so that they do not succumb to disintegration.

As at previous stations, we begin with theology. "Therefore, whether you eat or drink, or whatever you do, do all to the glory of God" (1 Cor. 10:31). We're used to the idea of glorifying God with our mouth via praise and prayer, but glorifying God by what we eat and drink is less familiar to us. Yet, that's what the apostle teaches. Our food and drink choices can magnify God's glory or minimize it.

That's the biblical principle, but how do we work that out in practice? No book of the Bible provides a diet plan. That's where God's truth as discovered by science can help us again. Scientific research about the impact of food on our minds and moods not only can educate our consciences but also can strengthen our wills so that we better obey God's voice in 1 Corinthians 10:31.

## Food and Mind

We use our minds to learn about food, but food itself helps our minds to learn. In fact, our brains use more food than any other bodily organ, grabbing 50 percent of available glucose.[1] That's why skipping breakfast is so bad for us. Doing so may give us more time at work, but we end up doing less work as the brain is deprived of essential nutrients and vitamins. Tests on children found that sugary breakfast cereals undermine attention and memory, whereas toast, eggs, blueberries, and strawberries increase their cognitive scores and coordination. The antioxidants found in salads purge the brain of unhealthy chemicals, and fish oil not only strengthens the brain but also deters dementia. You may want to eat avocados before your next exam, as they not only lower blood pressure but also increase oxygen and blood supply to the brain.

A healthy diet isn't important just for our work and study; it's also vital for our spiritual lives. God generally works in our souls through our minds, through our brains processing words and sentences. Therefore, any food that impedes the brain also impedes our relationship with God, and anything

---

1. Most of the food statistics in this chapter are taken from Alan Logan, *The Brain Diet: The Connection Between Nutrition, Mental Health, and Intelligence* (Nashville: Cumberland, 2006). See also "Food and Mood," Mind.org, http://www.mind.org .uk/information-support/tips-for-everyday-living/food-and-mood/#.VvQQIZMrJTY; Sarah-Marie Hopf, "You Are What You Eat, How Food Affects Your Mood," *Dartmouth Undergraduate Journal of Science* (February 3, 2011), http://dujs.dartmouth .edu/2011/02/you-are-what-you-eat-how-food-affects-your-mood/#.VvQQ0JMrJTY; Joy Bauer, "Improve Your Mood with These Foods," *Today Health*, October 31, 2006, http://www.today.com/id/15490485/ns/today-today_health/t/improve-your-mood-these -foods/#.VvQPeJMrJTY.

that strengthens the brain should strengthen our relationship with God. Yes, we pray, "Give us this day our daily bread," and God usually answers with full shelves at the grocery store. But that's where our responsibility to glorify God with our choices kicks in. The quantity and quality of what we eat and drink will influence the quantity and quality of our intellectual and spiritual lives.

## Food and Mood

What we eat affects not only how we think but also how we feel. Although some of our emotions flow from our thoughts, food also directly influences the production of mood-influencing chemicals in our bodies. I see this regularly and vividly in the life of my diabetic daughter. I can almost calculate her blood sugar and insulin levels by her emotions. But we don't need to be diabetic to experience the way some foods make us cranky and irritable whereas others make us energetic and happy. Scientists are helping us to understand these connections better, as PET scans can actually trace the way certain foods affect different parts of our brain, producing different emotions. For example, they've found that soluble fiber foods (e.g., oatmeal, strawberries, peas) slow down the absorption of sugar into the blood, reducing mood swings. The chemicals that make our brains function efficiently (neurotransmitters) are multiplied by foods such as walnuts, salmon, and those rich in vitamin D. Eskimos and other fish-dependent communities experience much lower rates of depression. On the other hand, junk food raises stress levels, and a deficiency of folate (found in lentils and broccoli) is common in depressed women.

When we're down or stressed, it may be that we need to read more of our Bible; but it may also mean that we need to eat better food. No amount of Bible verses will neutralize the basic nutritional rules that God has built into his world.

## Medications

I never dreamed that I would be on antidepressant medication. I was a naturally cheerful and optimistic person. And, more importantly, I was a Christian with a strong faith in God. But the day came when I was able to recognize that such medication was a God-given provision for me. That morning, I had once again awoken in a terrified state at 5:00 a.m., and I realized that I was fast losing a mental battle. In fact, there was no fight left in me. My mind was broken, and in my extremity it became clear that I had to seriously consider antidepressants, despite my initial resistance and reluctance.

While practicing medicine, I had sometimes prescribed antidepressant medication for others. But for me? Inconceivable. God, though, had brought me to this point of desperation, where I felt like I was drowning. At that point medication was a life belt he placed in front of me, and that day I took my first Citalopram 20mg tablet. Today, I thank God for his gracious mercy and provision. In fact, I doubt that I would have been able to write this book with David had I not given up my pointless struggle against God's kind providence and humbly accepted and used one of God's means of healing.

Obviously, this is a controversial topic, with the medical and Christian communities still learning about these drugs, when they should be used, and what role they should play in the lives of believers. What I'd like to do is share with you some of the lessons I've learned, as both a careful prescriber and a cautious consumer of them, to help you decide whether your depleted mind might benefit from medical replenishment.

*Don't rush to take antidepressants*. Medication should rarely be the first option, unless the situation is desperately bad. The majority of patients I saw who were dealing with emotional issues did not require medication. Often, people's emotional upheaval is temporary and can be resolved with understanding, family support, pastoral care, counseling, addressing detrimental lifestyle choices, and repenting of any sinful habits. There are many other things we should do before resorting to medication—the very things we saw at the earlier Refresh stations.

*Don't rule out antidepressants*. Although we shouldn't rush to medications, and we should usually try other healing means first, we shouldn't rule them out. Ask yourself if your refusal to even consider them might be sinful pride, false presuppositions, or an unbiblical and oversimplistic anthropology. On the latter point, if we deny the existence of mental or emotional disorders, we may be denying the Bible's teaching about the extensive, damaging effects of the fall upon our whole humanity. We know from the Bible that our body's physics, chemistry, and electricity are damaged by humanity's fall into sin. We know from science that our brains use physics, chemistry, and electricity to process thoughts and produce emotions. If we put these two facts together, we will understand how our brain's ability to process our thoughts and emotions will be impeded depending on the degree to which our brain is affected by the fall. Biblical anthropology helps us understand the damage the fall has done to our bodies, and also receive God's provision to reverse the damage.

*Don't wait too long*. The most important note to strike in the American culture of overprescription is "Don't rush to medication." However, waiting too long can also be harmful.

Occasionally, I have prescribed medication sooner rather than later because I felt the situation was extremely urgent and the depression worryingly deep. The farther down a hole someone falls, the harder the climb back up. And some were even close to suicide. My job at times was akin to a lifeguard grabbing hold of a drowning child. Only after rescue and stabilization could they even begin talking about how they got there, how to fully recover, and how to prevent its happening again.

*Don't expect rapid results.* Most modern antidepressants take ten to fourteen days to begin to make a noticeable difference and about six weeks before their beneficial effect can be fully evaluated. There may be some trial and error involved as the doctor tries to pinpoint the medication that works best for you in the right dosage.

*Don't rely on medication alone.* One of the biggest mistakes people make is thinking that just popping a pill will do the trick. I've never seen anyone recover from depression or anxiety by just taking medication. That's because there is usually a range of issues that need to be addressed. Medication can only work well when it's part of a holistic package of care that addresses our whole humanity.

*Don't dwell on side effects.* As with most drugs, some people can experience unpleasant side effects from antidepressants, and this should definitely be weighed in coming to a decision about them. But so should the side effects of doing nothing. Consider especially the side effects on your loved ones if you continue in your present state, perhaps for many months or years. Consider also that some of the most recent research has found increasing evidence that the longer depression goes on, the more damage is done to the brain, other organs, and even our bones. Summing up the loss of or damage to brain tissue, Dr. Philip Gold of the NIH Clinical Center said: "There's more loss of tissue in depression than there is in Parkinson's disease!" And "depression is a full-blown disease," he warned, "a systemic full body disorder with neurodegenerative aspects and is a progressive disease, much more serious, I think, than we had previously appreciated."[2]

Depressed and anxious people are susceptible to further anxiety over possible side effects, even more so if they are already prejudiced against antidepressants. Too often, this prevents them from taking medication as prescribed, taking too small a dose, and concluding too readily that "it didn't work."

Contrary to what some people claim, most antidepressants do not change your personality or somehow make you spiritually insensitive. God gave me my personality back by means of antidepressants, among other things. Are my emotions still intact? Of course they are. But what has gone is the emotional maelstrom of depression. I no longer feel like crying every time I hear something bad or crowd my mind with every sad thing there is to think about. Doing so was unhealthy and pathological. God has calmed the storm, partly through medication.

*Don't hold anything back.* Tell your doctor everything, and let him or her decide what's relevant. Don't minimize or ignore anything, even if it is embarrassing to share. Your doctor sees many people in your situation every week.

*Don't obsess about getting off antidepressants.* One of the first questions people ask when they start antidepressants is, "When can I stop taking them?" It's a bit like taking Tylenol

---

2. Philip Gold, "Can Depression Be Cured? New Research on Depression and Its Treatments," Library of Congress, http://www.loc.gov/today/cyberlc/feature_wdesc.php?rec=7417&loclr=eanw.

for your influenza symptoms, and the moment your temperature comes down you say, "Okay, I'm fine now. When can I go to work?" One of the lessons God teaches in depression is patience. Influenza takes its course, and you will be fine in a week or two. Depression also takes its course, but you need to be thinking six months to a year. Angst about wanting to get off meds as soon as possible only creates additional mental aggravation, which can prolong your depression. A common cause of depression relapse is coming off antidepressants before full healing has taken place.

*Don't come off medication too rapidly.* Although modern antidepressants are nonaddictive, it's still best to come off them in a planned, slow, graduated manner. Trust your doctor's wisdom and timetable as he guides you through a staged reduction of medication over a period of time. If the depression has been especially deep and long, some of the damage will not be fully reversed and will require ongoing antidepressants for a longer period.

I tried to come off medication completely quite a few times, and it usually went well initially. But after several months, I could feel all the old fearful symptoms returning. Through this personal experience and through hearing this story from too many people, I have learned to accept that just as David is on a small dose of Coumadin for the rest of his life to help prevent blood clots in his lungs, and just as my diabetic daughter will need daily insulin for the rest of her life to control high blood sugars, so I need some antidepressant to prevent mental and emotional breakdown. As Dr. Martyn Lloyd-Jones put it: "It is no more sinful to take drugs to put right the chemistry of the brain, than it is to substitute for the abnormal chemistry of the pancreas in a diabetic case by the use of insulin."[3] He went on:

> We can, therefore, reassure those who believe that it is sinful to take drugs which relate to brain function that, where clinical trial and proper use have shown them to be valuable, they should be received with thanksgiving. All things in nature and scientific knowledge are the gifts of God and should be used to his glory. . . . To accept and use them makes no difference to our faith and salvation.[4]

That kind of reasoning helped me accept my situation as God's sovereign providence (and kind provision). It also helped me to think of how the damage caused to a vehicle by unhealthy fuel is permanent. Sometimes the vehicle's engine has a lifelong problem processing fuel efficiently. Similarly, depression that has left us permanently scarred or which is genetic may need to be helped with antidepressants over our whole lives. However, God uses it like he used Paul's thorn in the flesh to teach us our weakness and God's strength.

*Don't be ashamed of taking antidepressants.* Yes, as with all of God's gifts, some misuse antidepressants, but that doesn't mean you shouldn't use them at all. If medications are a good gift of God, we ought not to despise them. A grace-paced life accepts all of God's graces when they are needed. Jeni admitted, "It was a struggle for me to accept the need for medication because I felt I was just succumbing to weakness and wasn't strong enough. And it was very difficult because a

3. Martyn Lloyd-Jones, *Healing and the Scriptures* (Nashville, Thomas Nelson, 1988), 169.
4. Ibid., 172.

lot of my family feels that you can't resort to medication. But I now view it as God's gift."

Ask for God's blessing upon medication and view it as part of a package of spiritual, physical, mental, and social measures. Sheila Walsh, the Christian singer who has also suffered from depression, says this: "I still take my medication. I take it each day with a prayer of thanksgiving that God had made this help available to those of us who need it."[5] To this I put my amen! My friend Sally, whose family has a history of bipolar disorder, contrasted her grandmother's lengthy hospitalizations after her children were born, which were very hard on all the other children and her husband, with her own experience of avoiding this separation from her newborns though the gift of lithium.

*Don't tell everyone.* If you decide medication is God's will for you, be careful whom you tell. Although taking most medications will elicit sympathy and prayer from the church, there is still a lot of misunderstanding around drugs for depression and other mental health problems. As you don't want to add argument and debate to your life as you struggle, carefully select those whom you tell, request that they keep it confidential, and ask them to pray for you and for God's blessing on the medication.

*Don't believe the caricatures.* Some people think only losers and lazy people get depressed. Nothing could be further from the truth. The vast majority of depressed Christians I've counseled over the years have been the exact opposite: type A personalities, high achievers always on the lookout for opportunities to serve others. So hyper, in fact, that they've

---

5. Sheila Walsh, "The Church and Mental Illness," SheilaWalsh.com, September 2, 2013, http://sheilawalsh.com/the-church-and-mental-illness/.

overdone it and broken down. But they're eager to get well and get back on track again.

Good food refuels our bodies and minds; in serious situations, medication stimulates additional brain fuel. Now let's identify activities that drain our energy and those that refill our tanks.

### Energizers

In our teens and twenties, we often seem to have unlimited reserves of energy. Nothing stops us or even slows us down. However, when we get into our thirties and forties we notice that our energy supplies are not infinite as we thought. Some days we fly, but other days we flop. What makes the difference? At first it's difficult to figure out, but eventually we notice that some activities fill our tanks while others drain us. Then we figure out that we have to balance fillers and drainers so that when we engage in a draining activity, we follow it with something that fills us. Otherwise we'll be running on fumes, which won't last long. Managing our energy consumption is as important as managing our money and our time. Pastor Greg's words reflect on his wife Jeni's experience of depression, but they are applicable to all Christians living long-term overstressed lives:

> The life of a young family can be incredibly stressful, and I don't think we really appreciate enough the weight of that day-in, day-out stress. And it doesn't have to be a family that experiences some really traumatic event. It can just be the normal everyday life of a busy young family. If you don't take precautions for physical health, emotional health, spiritual health, eventually you'll just run out of

gas and energy and you'll crash. And I think it's a real danger in conservative Christian circles that we just keep going, going, going, doing the Lord's will, having all the spiritual rationale behind it, and then suddenly finding ourselves completely exhausted.

Managing our energy begins with identifying our drainers and fillers so that we can plan ahead and fill up when we're running low. To help you identify yours, here's a sample of mine:

*Fillers*: Bible reading and prayer; listening to Christ-centered sermons and participating in church fellowship; reading books (mainly biographies and nonfiction, especially Christian); reading blogs; time with David and family; good food; doing yardwork; walking by rivers, lakes, and oceans; fishing; catching up with friends over coffee and distant family on FaceTime; hosting my kids' friends; seeing someone's conversion to Christ; witnessing growth in God's people; practicing gratitude; and laughing.

*Drainers*: Grocery shopping; handling family dental and doctor appointments; intervening in kid squabbles; overstretching my to-do list; fear and anxiety; overcommitting; counseling; oversocializing; staying up too late at night; watching daily news; emailing; dwelling on my failures; negativity; and managing administrative tasks.

Remember that we're all different. What fills me may drain you, and vice versa. I'm more of an extrovert while David is more of an introvert. We've learned to understand that what energizes me can be a major drain on him, and we respond accordingly. While grocery shopping drains me, one of my friends thrives on it and fights her husband to do it. Quite a few of my friends are refueled by singing God's praises together at their weekly choir practice.

Also, these are just the everyday drainers and fillers, the kinds that we encounter in our ordinary, day-to-day lives. Sometimes, though, our lives are hit with major changes such as the loss of a loved one, a family conflict, or a relocation. These punch major holes in our tanks, and we need to take extra-special care during such seasons.

Third, some drainers are so big and serious that they call us to reevaluate our situation. One pastor's wife who had a terrible experience at her last church describes it this way:

> We were in it, we were wholehearted about the mission of the church, but as the "behind-the-curtain" situation continued to be revealed to us, there was this constant sense of "there has to be another way." Finally, we realized that "other way" wasn't going to happen, and *we* needed to be the ones to leave and make a change.

Fourth, there are some activities that could go on both lists, what I call "double listing." That's because though some things fill us in one way, they may drain us in other ways. Although socializing replenishes me, it also depletes me. I love to spend an afternoon with other women and families, but by the time I get home to fix supper, clean up from the meal, and catch up with my teens, I'm mentally and emotionally good for nothing. That's why, earlier in the day, I have to set aside time to just chill, or do it early the next morning. I also have to pace my socializing and avoid putting a social opportunity on my calendar every day. Otherwise I will spend my summer days running on low fuel and become emotionally fragile.

Here's how a friend of mine describes her experience of double listing:

> I am an extrovert. I love being with people, inviting them to our home and getting to know new people. However, if I do this too many days in one week, I am in trouble! I will have a mini crash the next day. I need to also plan ahead with occasional naps, especially if it's going to be an evening event. Then I take a few "down days" where I do very little socializing.

Another example of double listing is physical exercise—it obviously drains me at the time, and for an hour or so afterward, but the net effect is a huge boost of physical and mental well-being.

Fifth, while I've highlighted the most significant daily fillers and drainers, we need to remember that everything, no matter how small, has an impact on us. It can be a hundred little things that turn our energy tanks into sieves and slowly drain us dry. That's why we need to refill every day, not just once a year on a short vacation.

Sixth, while we can try to eliminate or minimize some of the drainers, others are important responsibilities that are a vital part of our calling. We cannot and should not try to escape these but rather make sure we compensate for them when they arise. None of us should feel guilty about filling our energy tanks if it's with a view to serving God and others better.

Finally, I would add one essential filler: a daily, personal understanding of God's clear calling for you and a wholehearted, contented embrace of that vocation. Whether that's in the home or in the workplace, view your calling as designed by God especially for you, with a view to maximizing your own spiritual growth and usefulness. That will keep you persevering through the tough days and fill up your tank when other energy supplies are scarce.

We now leave station 8, having refueled with good nutrition and energizing activities. We've plugged some holes that were draining us, and, if our burnout was serious enough, some of us have also taken on emergency supplies of medication. But the gym is much more fun in good company, so let's run over to station 9 and add some important relationships to the mix.

# Relate

C

When my kids ran on a cross-country team, I noticed how the team spirit generated an energy and strength that they had found difficult to match when running alone. When I trained, I felt I could run much farther and feel less tired if someone else ran with me. On my own it could be a grind, and I needed much more willpower. That human connection and shared aim made all the difference. The advantage of being part of a team was powerfully illustrated in a movie my kids and I recently watched called *McFarland, USA*. Amazon describes it this way:

> In the tradition of Disney sports movies comes *McFarland, USA*, based on the inspiring true story of underdogs triumphing over tremendous obstacles. This heartwarming drama follows novice runners who strive to build a cross-country team under Coach Jim White (Kevin Costner) in their predominantly Latino high school. Everyone has a lot to learn about each other, but when Coach realizes the

boys' exceptional running ability, things change. Beyond their talent, it's the power of family, commitment to each other and work ethic that transform them into champions—helping them achieve their own American dream.[1]

In the movie, one team member was far from athletic, even considerably overweight, but through courage, determination, hard work, and, especially, supreme team spirit, he secured victory for the kids. It was an inspiring model of how we as Christians can relate to and support one another in the race of life.

Even in God's perfect world, we needed one another (Gen. 2:18). How much more today with a fallen humanity in a fallen world? Yet so many of us still try to live largely independent, solitary, disconnected, and self-sufficient lives. The result, as God predicted, is "not good."

God's answer to this "not goodness" was marriage. However, there are other important relationships that God has provided for our support and enjoyment. Join me at the Relationship station of Refresh Gym for some team-building exercises in five vital relational areas: with God, with our husband, with our children, with our friends, and with older women. Even if we just get that *order* of priorities right, it will make a massive difference.

## Relationship with God

If you've been putting this book into practice up to this point, you should find yourself with increased time and energy for your relationship with God. And it works the other way too.

---

1. https://www.amazon.com/McFarland-USA-Blu-ray-Kevin-Costner/dp/B00UMHRXYM.

A healthy relationship with God helps to increase time and energy. How so? Well, spending time with God gives us a new and healthier perspective on our lives and priorities. We see more clearly where we are to focus our efforts and what we can let go with a good conscience. Anxiety levels are also decreased through time in our heavenly Father's presence, releasing mental and emotional energy for other activities. Embracing more of his grace enables me to live a more grace-paced life. So how do we make the most of this time with the Lord? Following are some practices that have helped me over the years.

*Guarded time.* I try to treat personal Bible reading and prayer time as if it's an appointment on my calendar—not a dentist's appointment, but more like a friend I love being with. I get up half an hour before the kids, grab my cup of tea, and meet with God before I encounter anyone else. That's my ideal. When I was nursing babies, I often had to read and pray while nursing or wait for a quieter moment of the day.

*Undistracted mind.* In a survey of eight thousand readers, the Desiring God website found that 54 percent check their smartphones within minutes of waking up. More than 70 percent admitted that they check email and social media before their spiritual disciplines.[2] I agree with Tony Reinke, who commented, "Whatever we focus our hearts on first in the morning will shape our entire day." That's why I have resolved not to check email, social media, or the news before my devotional time, as I want to bring a mind that is as clear and focused as possible to God's Word.

---

2. Tony Reinke, "Six Wrong Reasons to Check Your Phone in the Morning, and a Better Way Forward," Desiring God website, June 6, 2015, http://www.desiringgod.org /articles/six-wrong-reasons-to-check-your-phone-in-the-morning.

*Varied devotions.* I like to alternate between Old Testament and New. I read through a Bible book, usually a few verses or a section at a time. I don't read huge chunks of Scripture, because I like to think through what I have read and meditate upon it. I'll often reach over to the bookshelf for Matthew Henry's commentary to get added insight. Sometimes I'll try to memorize a verse and revisit it later in the day. Let me emphasize that this is my personal system. You will have your own system. What matters is that you are connecting daily with the Lord in his Word.

*Podcasts and sermons.* In a guest blog post entitled "How a Busy Mom Can Stay Consistent in the Word," Courtney Reissig, author of *The Accidental Feminist: Restoring Our Delight in God's Good Design*, describes how she became intentional about reviving her relationship with God in his Word at a difficult stage of life:

> When I had my twins I didn't have a plan. I spent about six months not reading Scripture at all. I saw what that did to my life. I saw how much I needed God's Word in my life *regularly*. When I had my next baby I decided I was going to have a different plan. Because I'd already had kids, I knew that it was a little harder to get up in the morning or to read in the evening or to read midday during nap times. My plan was to listen to podcasts and sermons. I had God's Word coming in even though I couldn't crack open my Bible. Sometimes I read a psalm for the day. But I began to notice a difference in my soul simply because I changed my plan and had different expectations for myself. I can't do what I could do before. But I could do this. Ultimately, God is faithful. God is

faithful when we are intentional about knowing him through his Word.[3]

*Good sleep.* If I want to come to God's Word with energy and concentration, I need to get good amounts of sleep, in my case something like eight hours a night. The profit from my morning devotions is directly linked to my bedtime.

*Spiritual, Christ-centered books.* I love to see the greatness of Christ through books that teach theology in a practical way. For me, the key is substantive teaching that makes God great. I look for authors who are masters of efficiency with their words and crystal clear in their thinking and writing. Given my time limitations as a busy mom, these are important considerations when choosing a book.

*Daily reminders.* In order to maintain or recover communion with God through the day, I link regular daily habits with prayer or meditation. I may use a coffee break to pray, or I use particular situations to remind myself and my kids that God is ever present with us. One young woman related how she keeps a notebook to record all her favorite biblical or theological or other types of meaningful quotes, which she enjoys going back to and meditating upon.

*Accept imperfection.* Some of us suffer from an all-or-nothing tendency when it comes to our private devotional life: if we can't give God two hours, then there's no point in giving him anything. It's better to do a little regularly, though, than lots from time to time. Accept that at many stages of your life, you're just not going to be able to read the Old Testament six times a year. And remember, it's your

---

3. Courtney Reissig, "How a Busy Mom Can Stay Consistent in the World," July 6, 2016, https://www.crossway.org/blog/2016/07/how-a-busy-mom-can-stay-consistent-in-the-word/.

heavenly Father we're talking about. He's not standing there with a stopwatch.

## Relationship with Our Husband

How do I sum up twenty-six years of marriage in two pages? It's impossible, isn't it? However, what I thought I'd do is highlight the areas that have made the most beneficial difference in my marriage to David. However, before you try to implement any of these, it may be that you need to sit down with your husband, explain your sense of crisis, and make a plan to address the immediate need for margin in your family life. One Christian couple who hit the wall explained:

> One of the important things we did was sit down together as a couple. It wasn't just that she had to do some things; it was our whole family structure, our relationship. As a family we had to restructure everything. We had to slow the pace down. We couldn't do everything we thought we were going to be able to do. We both had to learn that. We needed to say no to people. And we have to realize that we can't do what others do. Some women can do more, and that's wonderful, but that's not going to set the bar for us.

Maybe you can ask your husband to read David's book for men, *Reset*, while you read this one. That will help him see things from a male perspective, which is a good start. But once you've had your "emergency summit," it's time to put some basics in place for the long term.

*Best friends.* David is my best and closest friend as well as my husband. There is nothing I would not consider sharing with him, and before all other friendships it is the one I cultivate most. We do go on regular date nights, but we equally enjoy one another's company at home. With young children, one of whom is diabetic, it was difficult to arrange babysitting in our early years in the US, as we had no extended family here. So we dated at home mostly. Now, it's easy for us to go out and leave an older child in charge for a few hours. It is important to remember that dating our spouse is more about spending regular, exclusive time together than about where we date. You don't have to go out for an expensive meal—for some families that option is not financially possible. One couple I know doesn't date at a restaurant, as they have a very large family. They send the kids to bed early and have a candlelit meal for two in their own cozy home. You can't beat that, especially if hubby gets to try out his culinary skills!

*Spiritual fellowship.* David and I try to talk daily about what God is doing in our lives and what he is teaching us through his Word and works. We did that from the first moment we met and have tried to keep it foundational throughout our years together. We discuss sermons we hear and try to talk daily about what we've discovered in our personal devotional times.

*Regular study.* After twenty-six years of marriage, it's hard to find marriage books that can teach us anything new. However, we always need to relearn old things again, and therefore we regularly read marriage books and articles and discuss them.

*Agreed roles.* David and I agree with the Bible's teaching about the different yet complementary roles God has designed for husbands and wives. However, what that looks like in practice can be quite challenging at times. We, therefore, try to regularly discuss our roles and responsibilities and try to resolve any areas of tension by prayerfully applying biblical principles to particular situations.

*Quantity and quality time.* It's frighteningly easy for husbands and wives to drift apart through spending too little time together. We marry someone we love to get more time with him and eventually end up seeing and speaking to him less frequently than when we were courting. Concerted effort is required to keep the flame burning, and there's simply no way to do that apart from spending time together. For us, that usually means we are both at home at least three or four evenings a week and spend a good hour each of these evenings talking together. We take the same day off each week to participate in family activities. We also make a point of taking our full vacation time and make sure that the congregation has someone to contact in case of emergency so that David does not need to be called back.

*Total transparency.* There's no area of David's life that I don't know about, and vice versa. We hold no secrets from each other but share everything, including bank accounts, Internet browsing history, and online passwords. We're not always checking up on each other, but knowing that we can at any time is just part of cultivating healthy accountability.

*Consistent bedtime.* David doesn't need as much sleep as I do, which means he rises an hour or so earlier. However, we usually go to bed at the same time each night and close out the day with joint prayer.

*Lots of laughter.* It's not just science and proverbial wisdom that tells us cheerfulness is good medicine (Prov. 17:22). We've proven it true in our marriage too. Even when David has had serious church troubles or I've struggled with an issue at home or work, one of us works hard to lighten the atmosphere.

*Vital vocabulary.* The most important words in any marriage are *please, thank you, I'm sorry, I forgive you,* and *I love you.* We try to say them as often as we can.

## Relationships with Our Children

As with marriage, there are numerous excellent books on parenting in general, and motherhood in particular, which I encourage you to read.[4] Instead of simply duplicating what's available elsewhere, I've provided below a quick list of the most joy-generating lessons I've learned (after much trial and error) in my relationships with my children.

*God's love.* I am called to represent God's love to my children. As the most visible representative of God in their lives, God's reputation in their minds depends on my providing a faithful image of God to them. That includes the grace of loving acceptance as well as the grace of loving discipline.

*Work-life balance.* Although mothering is busy, I have to be careful to avoid making it all-consuming. Yes, chores need to get done, but not at the cost of our relationship with our children. Yes, the family needs to be financially secure, but not at the expense of our children. Whatever our calling, we need to spend time with our kids without an agenda, time other than simply being there with them. It means that if my older sons whom I haven't seen all day come home and sit on the sofa to chat, I will drop what I am doing and sit with them. We usually enjoy tea or coffee as we chat about their day and

---

4. For example, Gloria Furman, *Treasuring Christ When Your Hands Are Full: Gospel Meditations for Busy Moms* (Wheaton, IL: Crossway, 2014); Rachel Jankovic, *Loving the Little Years: Motherhood in the Trenches* (Moscow, ID: Canon Press, 2010).

mine. These are precious times when we can reconnect, share, and become more prayerful for one another. Our home is the communication center for our kids. It's where they know they are safe and loved and prayed for. But for that to happen, I have to *be* home—not all the time, but most of the time.

As I consider my struggle with busyness over the years, I have often wondered what impact my excessive pace has had on my kids. Running from soccer game to grocery shopping, to dental appointment, to quick supper, to church meeting leaves little time for true communication. Poor communication fosters poor relationships. Will my kids grow up to be even busier than I, or will they learn that there is an alternative grace-paced way to live? God has opened David's eyes and mine to see that we must live that alternative before their eyes. That is why we have made it a priority in recent years to foster our family relationships above all other human relationships and to slow down our pace.

We may think our children want more action or more stuff, but what they really want is you and me. I love to sit with my younger teenagers and listen to their joys and woes. It binds us together. It also fosters life questions and discussion in a more natural way than any of us can get from a book.

I love to lift my four-year-old onto my lap and hug him. I love to listen to him as he blathers passionately about his own little world, and I pretend it all makes perfect sense. I know these moments are passing, and I savor them. My children are growing up, and soon they will move on. I want to enjoy and immerse myself in their lives as long as I can, and I pray that God will bless to them what is godly and hide from them my sinful failings.

*Gospel.* In addition to ensuring that my kids hear the gospel of grace preached each week in our church, I try to live it out in our daily lives. I encourage them to confess their sins and seek forgiveness, and I try to model that forgiveness when they sin against me. I make sure they know that my love is not conditional upon their exam marks or sporting success. I point them to the Holy Spirit's willingness to empower them in their fight against temptation.

*Humility.* When I sin against my children, I tell them I'm sorry and ask for their forgiveness. Children are forgiving if we are willing to admit when we have gotten it wrong.

*Patience.* My son went through Marine Corps boot camp, and in three months he and his fellow soldiers were turned from sassy teens to respectful, submissive young men ready to fight as part of a much bigger entity than themselves. But we must not make our homes like boot camp. When our older kids were young, we thought we had it all figured out. However, we soon discovered that their sinful natures and ours needed divine power to bless our mere human efforts. We learned patience, and we learned a lot about God's love for us. We learned that raising our children involves regular daily reflection on God's character, and that patience, longsuffering, slowness to anger, and compassion are a vital part of that.

*Time.* Although it gets harder as the kids get older, and especially when they start working and get their own cars, we work really hard to ensure our kids are together with us for our evening meal and family worship. With five kids, it's not always possible, but eating and worshiping together are the basics of keeping our family together. We devote our days off to the children, and rarely do either David or I go off and do our own thing. In the winter we organize family ski trips, and we bought a small boat for spring and fall fishing trips. We've spent a lot of money on family vacations over the years but never regretted a cent of it. The return on investment in terms of a stronger family is incalculable.

*Clarity.* Thanks to James Dobson's and Ted Tripp's books on parenting, David and I learned early in life the importance of setting clear boundaries for our children and also clear penalties if breached.[5] Although it seems counterintuitive, we've found that when we are consistent and courageous in our parenting, our relationships with our children thrive.

As I said earlier, there's no point in trying to do any work in these areas until you've gained some margin through implementing the previous stations of Refresh Gym. Otherwise, this will be just another overwhelming and impossible demand. However, I've found that when I have created margin in my life, parenting becomes a joyful filler of my heart rather than a miserable drainer of my energy.

### Relationships with Our Friends

Women in general are better at cultivating meaningful friendships than men. We seem to need it more and tend to thrive on it. But some women do struggle to make and maintain friendships.

Sometimes it's simply because we're too busy. We don't make the time for cultivating true and satisfying friendships. We always intend to, but we never get round to it. Other activities and responsibilities keep pushing it down our list of priorities. If we're honest, perhaps at the root of it is our pride, our sense of self-sufficiency that ignores or denies our

---

5. James Dobson, *The New Strong-Willed Child* (Carol Stream, IL: Tyndale, 2004); James Dobson, *The New Dare to Discipline* (Carol Stream, IL: Tyndale, 2014); Tedd Tripp, *Shepherding a Child's Heart* (Wapwallopen, PA: Shepherd's Press, 2011).

need of others. We may also be afraid of people getting to know us too well and discovering our faults and weaknesses. Or we may know others' faults and weaknesses, and we don't want to add another needy person to our lives. Our reluctance may perhaps be rooted in fear: "If I befriend Jill, what will Jennifer think? And Elaine?" And so on. Or it's possible that the number of those who need friends, on top of those you'd like to befriend, are so many that you feel paralyzed: "If I can't be friends with everyone—and I can't—what's the point of even starting?"

## Making Biblical Friendships

So how do we overcome these obstacles and begin to nurture nourishing friendships? We must begin with prayer. So often, we have not because we ask not (James 4:2). Pray that the Lord would show you your need of friends and that he would guide you to the right ones. Pray for the time, energy, and enthusiasm to pursue friendships. Pray that any friendship would be mutually beneficial, so that each person is being filled rather than its being one-sided.

Why not make a study of the subject to help you understand the Bible's teaching on friendship? If you do, you'll discover that friendship is at the very heart of God as each of the three persons of the Godhead relates intimately with one another. While on this earth Jesus was known as the friend of sinners in general, but he cultivated special friendships of increasing intensity with twelve men, then three men, and finally one very special friend. The more we study Christ's grace-motivated and grace-maintained friendships, the more we will model his wisdom, patience, kindness, and forgiveness in our friendships.

Three books I'd recommend are *The Company We Keep: In Search of Biblical Friendships* by Jonathan Holmes; *Messy Beautiful Friendship: Finding and Nurturing Deep and Lasting Relationships* by Christine Hoover; and *The Friendship Factor: How to Get Closer to the People You Care For* by Alan McGinnis.[6] The latter makes the point that unless we make healthy friendships a stated priority, they won't happen. A single woman told me that this is especially important for women like her: "We have no spouse to notice and warn when we are on the edge. Very few, if any, realize how close I am to burnout and the sometimes extreme pressure I put on myself to live up to the perceived standards of God's will and people's demands."

Now, you may be saying, "I know I should prioritize friendships, but I'm already squeezed dry. How can I add another to-do to my life?" That's the wrong way to look at it because good friendships don't deplete us; they renew us. Friendships reduce depression and improve our immune systems.[7] Harvard researchers found a strong connection between success and the amount of love enjoyed in life.[8] Psychotherapist Alan McGinnis said that if people used the restoring power of friendship, therapists would go out of business![9] Conversely, loneliness has been linked to an elevated risk of heart disease, stroke, cancer, and shortened life.[10]

---

6. Jonathan Holmes, *The Company We Keep: In Search of Biblical Friendship* (Hudson, OH: Cruciform Press, 2014); Christine Hoover, *Messy Beautiful Friendship: Finding and Nurturing Deep and Lasting Relationships* (Grand Rapids, MI: Baker Books, 2017); Alan McGinnis, *The Friendship Factor: How to Get Closer to the People You Care For* (Minneapolis: Fortress Press, 2003).

7. Matthew Edlund, *The Power of Rest: Why Sleep Alone Is Not Enough*, (New York: HarperCollins, 2010), Kindle ed., loc. 2275.

8. Ibid., 18–19.

9. McGinnis, *The Friendship Factor*, 95.

10. Ibid., 8–9.

Friendship may involve meals, playing sports, helping with practical problems, sharing family joys and sorrows, and taking an interest in each other's jobs. But the best friendships have spiritual growth at the core. Each friend thinks about how to help the other make spiritual progress. Each asks questions such as: "How can I pray for you? What temptation are you struggling with? What have you been learning in your Bible? What good books have you been reading?" I've shared some wonderful hours with a friend who has a similar interest in the kind of books I read. We have enlivened each other spiritually, and she has given me great insights into raising children, as some of hers are a bit ahead of mine. As both our husbands are pastors, we shared aspects of that calling on our lives too.

A younger friend, Emily, told me, "There is nothing I love more than having a good, long conversation with a brother or sister in Christ, whether that be my parents, my sister, my friends, my pastors, my mentor—you name it! I love talking about God's Word and his church, and feel so refreshed walking away from a profitable and substantial conversation."

We also need to recognize the changing nature of friendships, as our expectations may be rooted in a different age and culture. Emily Lanagan, communications professor at Wheaton College, has noted that due to a more fragmented and mobile society, and also the increased involvement of parents in school sports, friendships now have an average life expectancy of between five and eight years. In the past it was maybe more like thirty years.[11] When asked about her experience of the difficulty of friendships between married and single people,

11. Liuan Huska, "How to Keep Your Friends When Life Happens," *Christianity Today*, June 2016, http://www.christianitytoday.com/women/2016/june/how-to-keep -your-friends-when-life-happens.html.

her response highlighted the unfair one-sidedness that can sometimes deter such friendships:

> As I get older and have more friends whose kids are in late childhood and teenage years, they just don't have the flexibility that friendship demands. It is hard. Single people are often the ones asked to be flexible because the assumption is that we have the flexibility. "I have these demands, so can you accommodate me?" For me personally, it has been more gratifying and easier to be friends with older single people than with people my age who are married. When you're always the one doing the bending, at some point you just say, "I'm done."[12]

Friendship is really quite simple and shouldn't be over-complicated. William Rawlins, the Stocker Professor of Interpersonal Communication at Ohio University, noted that no matter if someone is only fourteen or as old as a hundred, the expectations for a close friend are the same: "Somebody to talk to, someone to depend on, and someone to enjoy. These expectations remain the same, but the circumstances under which they're accomplished change."[13] To encourage you, remember the words of the wise man who said, "Two are better than one" (Eccles. 4:9), and remember that bearing one another's burdens fulfills the law of Christ (Gal. 6:2).

### Relationships with Older Women

Cultivating relationships with older women in the church is something I have found to be hugely refreshing and spiritually

---

12. Ibid.
13. Julie Beck, "How Friendships Change in Adulthood," *The Atlantic*, October 22, 2015, https://www.theatlantic.com/health/archive/2015/10/how-friendships-change-over-time-in-adulthood/411466/.

edifying. No head knowledge, books, or chat rooms can substitute for life experience and the comfort and understanding that a mature Christian woman can bring to younger women. Such friendships are greatly encouraged in Scripture (Titus 2:3–5). I have sometimes gone to visit an older Christian woman with my heart laden with anxieties and come away refreshed and reorientated. Age brings perspective, and a fresh spiritual perspective can lift you up and get you going again.

Speaking of getting going again, after all these workout stations, are we not beginning to feel refreshed and reenergized, especially with a new support team of soul-strengthening relationships? So let's get back on the track and resume the race of life, this time grace paced rather than sprint paced.

# Resurrection

c

As I write, Easter weekend has just passed, and many Christians have reflected deeply on the resurrection of Jesus Christ. It has also been a time of reflection on my own "mini resurrection" from the depths of burnout and depression and the foretaste it has given me of the full and final resurrection.

I still have bad memories of the past. I was convinced I would never know joy in Christ again. Darkness and despair enveloped my mind and soul, and any hope of future joy and light seemed impossible. I remember a dark winter's day in Scotland, when the ocean raged, tossing up relentless mountains of dark waves of terror onto the rocks and shores, when the dark clouds hid every bright glow of nature from sight, and my mind and soul breathed that same ominous atmosphere. Black, bleak, hopeless. But then I recalled previous summer days, refreshing days, when that same ocean and sky glimmered with light and beauty, and nature rang out with color and beautiful sound as it breathed its energy from the sun. "If God can change such darkness to such brightness, then surely he can do the same for me," I thought. "If God can resurrect the dead winter landscape into a living array of green grass and gorgeous flowers, he can do that for me. If God can take seemingly dead trees and turn them into breathtaking canopies of green life, then surely he can do that for me."

And he did! Darkness and despair eventually gave way to new hope and new joy. Just like the psalmist in Psalm 107, my storm was indeed changed into a calm by his command. God used means: he brought me to Refresh Gym, taught me many lessons, and showed me a new way to live. Though the painful memories remain, they are fading, and the ultimate resurrection will erase the pain forever. You too can experience that same foretaste of the resurrection through God's blessing on your journey through Refresh Gym.

## New Pace

The Bible verse above the gym exit reads: "Do you not know that those who run in a race all run, but one receives the prize? Run in such a way that you may obtain it" (1 Cor. 9:24). The apostle Paul is teaching that there is a pace of running that will obtain the prize and a pace that won't. A sprint pace will not win a long-distance race, although that's what many of us try (and fail at). We try to run as fast as we can and even try to run everyone else's race for them too. What miserable bondage! Now, having passed through Refresh Gym, many of us have learned that we must follow God's race plan, a much more deliberate, grace-paced race, if we want to finish well.

There will be times when we have to run faster and push ourselves harder, but these times will be less frequent as we remind ourselves of the distance we have yet to run. These bursts of busyness and stress will be more frequently interspersed with refreshing recovery strategies, so that we will be much less likely to crash and burn as before. The occasional, sudden, immediate demands of our energy will not deplete us as before, because we have left margin in our lives.

## New Conscience

Initially, we can expect some difficulty as we slow our pace. It may be difficult because, in comparison with our pre-Refresh life, it seems lazy to be running slower, or we may feel guilty about reducing other commitments and taking breaks to renew our energy. When such false guilt creeps up behind us, runs on our shoulder, and whispers, "Faster!" in our ears, we educate our consciences with the biblical knowledge and understanding gained in Refresh Gym.

If we've always run fast, we may find our initial attempts at slowing the pace a bit of a struggle. Satan would have us believe that frantic-paced living is godly and that grace-paced living is not. He may even quote Scripture in the process: "Go to the ant, you sluggard" (Prov. 6:6). Often my conscience has struggled with this, and I have felt the pull into more service, faster service, everybody's service.

But God has taught me that, no, the grace-paced life is not only his will but more honoring to him. For me, to pace myself means less of my efforts and more of God's grace. I have had to learn to fight hard against unbiblical, false guilt and personal expectations. I have learned to look up to God before looking across to people and ask: "What does God want me to do right now?"

The key is to grasp that pacing ourselves is biblical, whereas living the fast, frantic life is not. It takes faith to believe that and to follow through with it. To live it is in fact a dying to self—a dying to our self-will, our self-sufficiency, and our self-image. Have you understood frantic living versus grace-paced living in that way before?

Jesus's mother, Mary, seemed in a hurry to get his ministry going when she brought to him the dilemma at the wedding at Cana of Galilee, but Jesus showed her that he was in no such hurry. He always waited on his Father's will, timetable, and pace (John 2:3–4). How much more must we wait on our heavenly Father's will, timing, and pace in every area of life?

### New Honesty

It is hard and humbling when we have to acknowledge weakness. It may fill us with anxiety to admit to our husband, kids, friends, coworkers, or coach that we have resolved to live a much more deliberate, grace-paced life. After all, who doesn't want to get going and get things done? How will I look? Will they think I am lazy?

I have found, however, that simply being honest and admitting my weakness and limitations has often been a relief. Sometimes it's been a relief to others too. Some may never understand why we are not running around responding to every request like we used to. However, I have been amazed at how many women open up with honesty about their own weakness and weariness following my admission. They too have made life-changing decisions, which have enabled them to live a more refreshing, grace-paced life.

### New Energy

I wish I had the energy and stamina I had thirty years ago, but I've had to accept the limiting effects of aging and bearing five kids and learn how to manage my energy wisely. Just as a battery-operated toy runs down if we leave it on, our energy will run down pretty fast. If we are careful to switch it off now and then, it will last longer.

I've often found myself with many useful activities and events to choose from in a given week. All good, but not all good for *me*. Previously, I would have tried to do each one, but Refresh Gym has taught me to make hard choices. Just as an athlete must choose a limited number of races to run in, we must pick our races, space them out, and allow recovery time. That way, we run with vigor and purpose instead of with lethargy and leaden legs. Our aim is to excel in a few areas rather than fail in many.

By paying attention to rest and refueling, both physically and spiritually, we avoid extremes of energy expenditure followed by exhaustion. We learn to relax without false guilt; learn to view sleep, exercise, and healthy regular eating as God's gifts; and learn to accept the help of others with humility when needed.

### New Joy

Many women I have known and counseled couldn't remember when they last had joy in living or serving. Fear, anxiety, dread, and despair had been their daily companions. They looked ahead to what was left of the race and feared they could never finish it. The thought of the next day, the next meal, the next customer, and the next email to answer was a miserable mountain to climb. No more laughter, no more joy. But God provided a way back to joy through Refresh Gym. Hope revived as they passed through each station. Fear was replaced with calm. Light broke through into the mind, body, and soul. Paralysis was replaced with purpose and a renewed sense of calling. Problems became opportunities. Moments of reflection became moments of worship. Renewed joy in their Bible reading and prayer rebuilt the hope of fullness of joy in the future.

## New Theology

As I look back on my life and conversations with other struggling women, a common thread has been evident—a wrong theology. Yes, we believed that God loves us and saved us by grace alone, and that we could not work our way into favor with God. Yet at times we slipped into the false thinking that God is a slave driver rather than our loving heavenly Father, who delights to see his children thrive.

Maybe we also viewed resting in Christ as a purely spiritual action, with no connection to physical rest or downtime. But when we obey our Creator's instructions for temple care, we will take breaks and go to bed on time, even with an unfinished to-do list. When we do that for these reasons, not only are we physically resting, but also we are resting in Christ. We are acknowledging and accepting our creaturely limitations. Contrary to what we may think, he is not disappointed in us for not finishing our list. Instead he is honored because we entrust what we cannot finish to him. We rest more in him and rely less on ourselves and our abilities.

Our drivenness was perhaps also fueled by the mistaken belief that anything less than burnout for the kingdom is not true service. Stories of martyrdom or missionaries and their wives dying in the most desperate human circumstances have been mistakenly viewed as the gold standard of Christian service. Yet, as we have seen, God's calling to each of us is unique, and he takes great delight in us when we serve him in it. He is highly honored when we work in the office, school, or home doing the most menial tasks out of love to him (Col. 3:23). He does not demand burnout. He rejoices to see us taking biblical care of the bodily temple he has gifted to us and is delighted when we live conscious of our weakness and in total dependence on his daily refreshing grace.

## New Team

As we leave Refresh Gym, one of our favorite Pauline verses is "I planted, Apollos watered, but God gave the increase" (1 Cor. 3:6). Previously we ran the race of life as if everything depended on us. Now we recognize that we need to run as part of a team. We need the support and encouragement of others. We need to be more vulnerable, admit our limitations, and ask for help. In so doing, we open doors of opportunity for others to serve the Lord in drawing alongside us, deepening relationships and growing friendships in the process. David and I can definitely identify with Greg and Jeni's post-depression discovery:

> This whole journey we've been on has been such a strengthening thing for our marriage. We've been more open with each other, we express our feelings more, and he's not afraid to open up to me, because he was kind of worried how I would react. It's really strengthened our marriage that we can be more honest with each other when we need a break, or I'm not feeling so well today. We rely on each other a lot more, look to help each other more, and look to God together more.

## New Sensitivity

Refresh Gym has made us more conscious of our inbuilt biological rhythms. We've become aware of the daily ebb and flow of energy, and the impact of sleep, food, friends, work, and play on our bodies, minds, and souls. We sense the emotional drains much sooner. We grasp the reality of soul weariness when we have pushed or indulged our bodies too far, when we have stayed up late too many nights or worked too many long hours. Instead of ignoring the warning signs, we heed them and embrace the loving God behind them and make the necessary adjustments. When the Word seems dry and concentration flitting, we go through our checklist of God's parameters for temple care and make adjustments where needed.

Not only are we more sensitive to our own spiritual, emotional, and physical warning lights; we are more sensitive to others' also. We now notice the pale, drawn face of a young mother who has lost her spark, the withdrawing of a student from all her church friends, or the short temper of a previously patient coworker. We have become much more sympathetic to frail humanity in all its complexities.

## New Resources

When a large rock goes through the ice, a new layer of ice begins to form over a number of days. Initially that ice is very thin and fragile, so if you attempt to stand on it too soon, you will go through it. That's what I did when I began to feel stronger. I reverted to my predepression pace, when suddenly I found myself back in the cold, icy waters I thought I had put behind me. I was initially panicked but then remembered

Refresh Gym and all the resources I had acquired there. I went back to the various stations and started to rebuild the "ice" using the various exercises. I now know what to do when I feel the ice cracking, and I'm also more careful about testing the new ice too soon.

## New Checkup

When I exercise, I take regular sips of water, even though I may not feel thirsty. If I forget, I spend the rest of the evening catching up with a raging thirst at the kitchen faucet. Far better to balance my exercise with much-needed water as I go along and so prevent dehydration. That's why we should regularly revisit Refresh Gym even when we're not feeling overwhelmed. At first, we should do it every week, then, as we get stronger, every month, and definitely at the first sign of trouble. We want to regularly check our pace before that overwhelmed feeling even begins to cast its ugly shadow.

## New Lens

As we look ahead, the future that had seemed so dark and depressing now looks much brighter and clearer because we have a new *focus* and a new *lens*. By clarifying our purpose and plan we are now focused on a few priorities rather than multiple aims. We know why we are running, where we are going, and how we will get there. We keep focused on these life purposes to keep us on track.

Refresh Gym has also taught us how to use the Word of God as a lens when reading scientific research that God has enabled scientists to discover. We use the lens of our biblical knowledge to filter out any research that contradicts God's

Word and to let in God's truth wherever he has put it.[1] So the Bible is not just what we read but what we read with, and it is such a good lens that it is sufficient to keep us from falling into error in this area.

## New Watchfulness

Life is short! This is not just a cliché but a growing reality for all of us. As far back as the age of nine, I was impressed with this when two school friends drowned. Yet, even then, time seemed to be a vast expanse ahead of me. Now I realize that each day is a rare and precious gift. What I choose to do with my time today matters a lot; I may not have tomorrow. That means I have to carefully watch for what is important today and especially for eternity. That goes a long way toward focusing my mind on the essentials and ditching the nonessentials.

## New Patience

We live in a quick-fix society that demands instant results. If we learn anything in Refresh Gym, it's that there are no quick fixes when it comes to depression, stress, or anxiety. Yes, we use the stations God has provided and take responsibility for what we can do, but we come to realize that it takes time for all these means to take root and become effective. This is how God teaches us patience. My physical and emotional recovery went quicker than my spiritual recovery, especially in the area of assurance, which sometimes frustrated me. It was during that time that I really grasped the sovereignty of God and patiently submitted to the wisdom of his timetable.

---

1. It was John Calvin who first used the illustration of spectacles to explain this. He said that the Bible is not only what we read but what we read with. John Calvin, *Institutes of the Christian Religion*, ed. John T. McNeill, trans. Ford Lewis Battles, Library of Christian Classics, vols. 20–21 (Philadelphia: Westminster, 1960), 1.6.1.

## New Balance

Try to imagine your life like a weekly financial budget. At the beginning of the week, each column is filled to capacity with the allotted amount of money. As the week goes by, we make spending choices that run down each column. If we overspend in the food column, we must reduce our spending ability in another column. If we continue spending and ignore the impact on each column, we will run into debt and be in financial trouble. Setting our budget correctly and implementing it is key to a good outcome and weekly "financial peace," as Dave Ramsey puts it.

Refresh Gym challenges us to balance the different columns in our life: devotional time, work time, family time, church time, exercise time, technology time, relaxation time, and so on. The challenge is to be realistic about our goals in these areas, ensure we maintain a healthy balance, and then stick with it.

## New Habits

When we first immigrated here, I had thirty days to get my Michigan driver's license. Can you imagine my horror as David brought home our new vehicle and the driver's seat was on the "wrong" side? It got worse when I had to take the wheel and start driving on the "wrong" side of the road. Instead of a stick shift, the car had an automatic transmission, and the van itself was a beast compared to anything I had driven before. I was faced with two choices: get the license or stay in the house with four kids every day. With that in mind, I got going. My left foot, previously so important for driving a stick-shift vehicle, was totally confused as to what to do. I couldn't just let it sit there doing nothing. Worst of all, on my first solo drive I took a wrong turn and ended up facing two lanes of oncoming traffic. Mercifully I survived and, through necessity and practice, it all became second nature—so much so, that the next time I went back to Scotland, it took some conscious effort to revert to my old way, on the "correct" side of the road. I couldn't find my left foot!

Putting into practice our newly discovered grace-paced lifestyle can initially be awkward and even discouraging. However, once we grasp that it is essential if we are to persevere in this race, and we put it into practice, we will learn to embrace and love our new way of living. If we are believers in Christ, we also have the powerful motivation of the Holy Spirit's help along the way.

## New Humility

It takes humility to admit our limitations and weaknesses, and even more to admit them to others and to seek help. Recently, one of my friends came out of a hard and long bout with anxiety. Although she had gathered a few tools for dealing with it over the years, this bout exhausted those quickly, and at last she sought out counseling. "I'm grateful for my church's openness about mental health and counseling," she wrote to me, "because even though there have been times in the past when I probably *should* have sought some outside help, this is the first time I have." Elizabeth Moyer describes the humbling relief of learning to substitute dependence for independence:

> The most stressful seasons in my life climax in a moment when I realize I can't do it all. I am reminded of my human finiteness and fallibility. Instead of losing my breath in

anxiety, I should be able to breathe a deep sigh of relief. I can't do it all, but I don't have to. I am not enough, but Christ is. If the Creator of the universe loves me enough to die and take away all my ugly sin, then he cares about the pressures of life that bear down on me daily.[2]

When we look back at the floor of Refresh Gym, we see a pile of weights we've discarded along the way: independence, self-sufficiency, self-confidence, indispensability, and invincibility.

## New Grace

Refresh Gym shreds our sweaty performance metrics and opens our hearts to receive more of God's refreshing grace. We receive more grace by refusing to turn this book on a grace-paced life into a new bunch of oughts, shoulds, and musts. Yes, there are many practical suggestions in this book, but don't turn self-care into further self-harm. Don't turn what should release you from bondage into another legalistic prison. Go slowly, go gradually, go grace-fully. Remember these liberating words of Jesus: "She has done what she could" (Mark 14:8). As Allan Mallinger explains in his book *Too Perfect: When Being in Control Gets Out of Control*, there is an important difference between perfectionism (everything must be perfect) and excellence (the healthy will to excel). Building upon Mallinger's distinction, we can distinguish between them in the following ways:

- Perfectionism is rigid; excellence is flexible.
- Perfectionism is self-defeating; excellence is health giving.

2. Elizabeth Moyer, "What Is a Biblical Response to Stress?," Institute for Faith, Work, and Economics, March 16, 2016, https://tifwe.org/a-biblical-response-to-stress/.

- Perfectionism never satisfies; excellence gives pleasure.
- Perfectionism is impossible; the desire to excel is usually possible.
- Perfectionism does not distinguish between performing heart surgery and washing dishes; excellence recognizes that some activities require more attention than others.
- Perfectionism views failure as catastrophic; excellence views it as part of learning.
- A perfectionist's sense of worth depends on perfect performance; excellence does not tie identity to performance.
- A perfectionist can see only what's lacking in a job or relationship; excellence sees what is good and enjoyable.

As Jerry Bridges puts it:

> Living by grace instead of by works means you are free from the performance treadmill. It means God has already given you an "A" when you deserved an "F." He has already given you a full day's pay even though you may have worked for only one hour. It means you don't have to perform certain spiritual disciplines to earn God's approval. Jesus Christ has already done that for you. You are loved and accepted by God through the merit of Jesus, and you are blessed by God through the merit of Jesus. Nothing you ever do will cause him to love you any more or any less. He loves you strictly by his grace given to you through Jesus.[3]

---

3. Jerry Bridges, *Transforming Grace* (Colorado Springs, CO: NavPress, 2014), 73. Quoted in Paul Tautges, "Freedom from the Performance Treadmill," *Counseling One Another*, March 19, 2016, http://counselingoneanother.com/2016/03/19/freedom-from -the-performance-treadmill-2/.

We not only *receive* more grace; we *give* more grace. Aware of our own weaknesses and frailties we extend more grace to others who are failing and falling.

## New Fruitfulness

Most women, myself included, know we need to make changes, but we fear reduced productivity. Let me take you to the garden to calm your fears. Vegetable growers know that it is important to thin out the young plants so that what you leave in the ground has space to mature and flourish into tasty, good-quality, nourishing vegetables fit for the kitchen table. At no point would you sit at the table bemoaning the tiny little shoots you had to remove to produce such a harvest. Let's apply that same principle to our daily productivity. Most women I have spoken to have found that far from achieving less, they have achieved more, especially in the realms of quality and satisfaction.

## New Christology

Whenever we fear that reducing our output from 120 percent to 100 percent means we're getting lazy, it helps to reflect on how Christ experienced limitation. As God, he had never known any limitation. As man, he experienced all the normal human limitations. If he can accept such a change in his limitations, how much more should we? Accepting and submitting to our limitations should draw us nearer to Christ and give us a new understanding of Christ's humanity. As Brad Andrews put it (with my additions in brackets):

> We can only rest in our limitedness when we see that Jesus limited himself by leaving the culture of the Trinity and

entering the culture of man for our sake. His act of incarnation and redemption settles our need for significance on this side of eternity. Healthy leaders [including women] accept their limits because when we look to Jesus, we see the ultimate limitation—God becoming flesh and blood to bring us spiritual rescue. And as we rest in this truth, we can let the unlimited One and his limitless grace give us courage to be the limited leader that we are and in the end, flourish for the good of our churches [and our families], and the gospel.[4]

## New Hope

We began our journey through Refresh Gym, downcast, discouraged, tired, and joyless. All we could see was failure as we trundled from one item on our to-do list to the next, and we felt like the prisoner in the freezing Siberian quarries just going from one icy rock face to the next. Frozen, cold, hopeless. Our life's race, far from looking like that of a confident runner about to receive a crown, looked more like that of the first marathon runner who dropped dead from exhaustion on delivering his message.

Now, having passed through Refresh Gym, we face the future with new hope and confidence. Grace has replaced grind. Joy has replaced joylessness. Having experienced a mini resurrection from burnout, we face the future with renewed hope.

We'd seen his power rescue us from our sins. We've now seen his power rescue us from the grave of burnout and transform us. Although we'll face future threats, we now know

---

4. Brad Andrews, "Limitless Grace for Limited Leaders," *For the Church*, February 29, 2016, http://ftc.co/resource-library/1/1933.

where to run, how to run, and above all to whom to run. Whatever he has done in the past, he can and will do again.

And when our tomorrows are over and the ultimate resurrection day dawns, he will raise us up to perfection. Our searching cries for our heavenly Father will be replaced with endless joyful embrace. We will no longer be burned out, but be burnished splendor at God's right hand! That's the horizon to keep in view—not the next diaper, or the next meeting, or the next business trip, or the next meal, but the next life.

Let's run, that we may be able to say: "I have fought the good fight, I have finished the race, I have kept the faith. Finally, there is laid up for me the crown of righteousness, which the Lord, the righteous Judge, will give to me on that Day, and not to me only but also to all who have loved His appearing" (2 Tim. 4:7–8).

# Acknowledgments

We want to thank the entire Crossway team for the opportunity to write this book and for all the help they have given us throughout the process. We're especially grateful to Justin Taylor for providing the creative impetus and to Lydia Brownback for her skillful editing that pushed us to a much better finished product. Above all, we're grateful to God for his grace in not only saving us, and not only bringing us through many deep waters and dark valleys, but for all the lessons he has taught us along the way and the way he has worked all things together for our good and his glory.

# General Index

# Scripture Index

# Also Available from David Murray

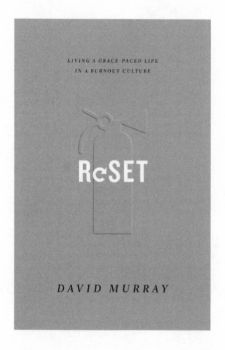

Although burnout is growing increasingly common among men, it doesn't have to be inevitable. Pastor and counselor David Murray offers men gospel-centered hope for avoiding and recovering from burnout, setting their lives to a more sustainable pace.

For more information, visit crossway.org.